Southern Baptist and Expository Preaching

Southern Baptist and Expository Preaching

Biblical Interpretation, Values, and Politics in Twentieth-Century America

BRENTON CROSS
Foreword by Sean Cotter

WIPF & STOCK · Eugene, Oregon

SOUTHERN BAPTIST AND EXPOSITORY PREACHING
Biblical Interpretation, Values, and Politics in Twentieth-Century America

Copyright © 2021 Brenton Cross. All rights reserved. Except for brief quotations in critical publications or reviews, no part of this book may be reproduced in any manner without prior written permission from the publisher. Write: Permissions, Wipf and Stock Publishers, 199 W. 8th Ave., Suite 3, Eugene, OR 97401.

Wipf & Stock
An Imprint of Wipf and Stock Publishers
199 W. 8th Ave., Suite 3
Eugene, OR 97401

www.wipfandstock.com

PAPERBACK ISBN: 978-1-6667-3217-7
HARDCOVER ISBN: 978-1-6667-2555-1
EBOOK ISBN: 978-1-6667-2556-8

12/01/21

Contents

Acknowledgments vii

Foreword by Sean Cotter ix

Author's Note xi

Chapter 1   Introduction   1

Chapter 2   Historical Development of Expository Preaching   11

Chapter 3   The Communal Role of Expository Preaching   51

Chapter 4   The Translation Methodology of the SBC   83

Chapter 5   Social Impact on Culture   112

Bibliography 139

Acknowledgments

I AM VERY THANKFUL to some very dear and significant people, who supported me and without whom this project would not have been completed. I am truly grateful for Dr. Sean Cotter, his consistent support and leadership has truly enabled me to remain focused and to pursue excellence in all my research and academic endeavors. I am also indebted to Drs. Daniel Wickberg, Frederick Turner and Eric Schlereth for their expertise and wise guidance. It is somewhat surreal that I have been able to complete this project. Both my mother and father were able to see me start this project but passed away and did not see me finish. This research journey was in part due to their investment in me and now I can say that I have finished what I started in loving memory of Mom and Dad. Finally, but most significantly I must thank Jessica, my wife, for her untold love and care during this project. She has been my joy, my consolation, and cheerleader.

    April 2019

Foreword

DR. BRENTON CROSS'S STUDY asks a question of fundamental importance for those who take the evangelical mission of Christianity seriously: how should we preach? If the Gospels charge Christian believers with not only the duty to live their lives well, in communion with God, but also the duty to express Christian beliefs, to convince others to adopt these beliefs, and to deepen the understanding of fellow believers, then preaching lies at the center of Christian practice. The way in which Christians preach is the way they live out their theological convictions. Debates over the nature of preaching, therefore, are debates over what it means, in fact, to be a Christian. Cross situates his examination of this question as much in theological terms as in historical analysis, examining the role of expository preaching within the Southern Baptist church. His careful attention to debates over styles of preaching ground his focus on the nature of Christian belief in the world. It is a study driven by scriptural indictment and scriptural conviction.

This gospel charge—in fact, the call of all of Christian Scripture—also lies at the center of Cross's answer to his question: How should we preach? The way Scripture directs us to preach. Cross argues that the study of Scripture reveals models for effective preaching. Tracing these models back to the prophets of Hebrew Scripture, Cross demonstrates a heavily exegetical model designed to bring the listener into a deeper understanding of the sacred text. This argument effectively uses a feedback loop, in which the preaching is modeled on scripture, and the scripture is the subject of the preaching. Following the work of Grant Osborne, Cross calls this method "expository preaching."

Cross's aim is both historical and polemical. He enters into a broad debate about the nature of preaching, scripture, and faith, a debate which pits expository preaching against less textual and less scholarly approaches. These other ways of preaching, he demonstrates, rely on emotional appeal rather than rational argument, immediate intelligibility rather than careful explanation, and personal anecdotes and jokes rather than the presentation of stories and parables from Biblical texts. In each alternative, the expository preacher opts to take his listener deeper into the scholarship of the text. This preference has a corollary in the approach to translation the book recommends: in place of a looser, more relevant "dynamic equivalence," Cross argues for a more rigorous "complete equivalence." This book makes the argument that a style of preaching modeled on Scripture should itself focus on unpacking the scriptural text, so that the listener may encounter the text more deeply. In other words, the expository preacher lives out the Gospel charge both in the content of his preaching and also in the method.

Like Christian belief, which aims to change the way people live in the world and the very nature of the world's relationship to God, the aim of expository preaching is also trained on the world. In Cross's account expository preaching embodies a conservatism that attracts those who value tradition and dogmatism to the Southern Baptist church. Cross demonstrates the connections between this style of preaching and conservative positions on social issues, such as gender roles. An evangelical mode of belief leads to engagement with the world, as the sermon's message guides the listener's outward-facing actions in the world. Thus, we can notice a continuance of the feedback loop, by which a biblical mode of preaching appeals to conservative values and simultaneously strengthens those convictions. In some of the most compelling work of the book, Cross is again polemical in his demonstration that, as strong as this feedback system intends to be, the Southern Baptist church has taken positions without the type of justification expository preaching should provide. In Cross's analysis, the SBC has occasionally "made up" its social positions, in the sense that he finds no scriptural basis for them. Instead, these seem to be guided by politics designed to appeal to conservative voters, rather than exegetical theology designed to teach and to guide conservative Christians. Throughout this study, Cross's preference is for the eternal over the contingent, for access to divine truth through Scripture over embrace of secular certainty, even when both of these positions appeal to the same conservative public.

The appeal of Cross's work lies in its emphasis on questions central to Christian belief and his willingness to make connections between belief and practice—scholarly practice, preaching practice, and one's life in the world. His work finds inspired combinations between the theological exegesis, the history of the Southern Baptist church, and the normative debates over social policy. In summary, we can appreciate this book's thorough treatment of the origins, history, value, and implementation of expository preaching. This book's account of preaching is worthy of the central role evangelism holds in Christian faith.

Sean Cotter
Professor of Literature and Translation Studies, The University of Texas at Dallas

Author's Note

Southern Baptist Expository Preaching Homiletic: Biblical Interpretation, Values, and Politics in Twentieth-Century America

THIS PROJECT ADDRESSED THE influence and role of the Southern Baptist (SB) expository preaching methodology by examining the role of expository preaching, its innate characteristics, and its espousal by SB pastors and theologians in the twentieth-century for influencing personal and social values and politics in the twenty-first century. My research begins with an investigation of the historicity that led to the development of the expository homiletic theory and delves into the historical concepts and intrinsic modes of thought and process foundational to expository preaching from the early first century of Christianity to the twentieth century. I demonstrate its advocacy by the SB theologians, pastors, and leaders in the formation of their biblical theology and social agenda. There are inherent characteristics in the expository method that underlie a proclivity toward or adherence to deeply embedded historical beliefs that were derived from the first century. This belief system pervades the preparatory and delivery aspects of the SB homiletic theory. The SB expositor has subscribed to a methodology that encompasses the consideration of a passage or text in a context which involves a study of the original biblical language, grammar, syntax, and cultural background of the text. The SB expositor attempts to didactically uncover the original meaning of the text based on its cultural context in order to communicate and disseminate divine truths that emanate from the text. The exposition typically involves an exegetical and hermeneutical method to uncover practical divine truths succinctly that will affect personal and societal change. My study includes an anthology of the sermonic material and homiletic practice of the foremost SB expositors, theorists, and homileticians. I explore the facets of their hermeneutical and homiletic processes to elucidate the basis of their adherence to their propositional and moralistic expository style which is shrouded in personal, political and social agendas. I delineate the basis for the perfunctory relationship between the translation methodology which SB theologians pursue and their acquiescence with the need for purity and literalness in understanding the original biblical texts written in Hebrew, Aramaic, and Greek. SBC theologians perpetuate a need for reading and preaching primarily based on the original text and replicating the exact words of God in the sermonic moment. SBC theologians desire to re-express the original tonal voice and images of the biblical text for twentieth and twenty-first century Bible readers. My analysis includes a demonstration of the influence of an exegetical, hermeneutic, and translation methodology that not only increases or builds the denomination but also affects social and political change. Furthermore, I have examined several works that have detailed the ideological and political conflicts between SB theologians, pastors, and leaders in an effort to show their approach and impact among the SB and their level of effectiveness in national and social arenas. I assert that the Southern Baptist support of expository preaching has emboldened and furnished both practitioners and congregants with a historical methodology in which they reproduce and propagate divine truths to bring about personal, social, and political change.

Chapter 1

Introduction

THE SOUTHERN BAPTIST CONVENTION (SBC) evolved from a missionary organization that was primarily concerned with the mobilization of evangelism locally and internationally into a denominational body that both funded missions and perpetuated conservative social values through literal translation, exposition, and adherence to the Bible. This evolution was so successful that by the twenty-first century the SBC had approximately sixteen million members nationwide.[1] The issues that the SBC supported were based on hermeneutical, homiletic, theological, and translation theory, represented as their scriptural interpretation philosophy. These issues included social ideologies such as anti-abortion, anti-gay rights or gay marriage, conservative entrepreneurial "supply side" economics, and even freedom of religious expression in public institutions. The framework for interpreting and communicating the Scriptures was termed "expository preaching." In expository preaching, the pastor or theologian focuses predominantly on the content and context found in the biblical text under consideration. The expositor engages in historical study of the background of the text to ensure an interpretation of the text aligns correctly with historical context. The exposition is used for a thematic and theological message within a historical and biographical discourse that becomes expositional in nature. The expositor may focus on a single verse, full sentence, or paragraph of biblical text. Expository sermons in reality can be based on any length of biblical text.

---

1. Southern Baptist Convention, "Fast Facts."

Purpose of the Study

This project is a study of the influence and role of the SB (Southern Baptist) expository preaching methodology. Its purpose is to examine the role of expository preaching, its innate characteristics and its espousal by the SBC (Southern Baptist Convention) in the twentieth-century to effect personal and social values and politics in the twenty-first century. I assert that SB support of expository preaching has emboldened and furnished both practitioners and congregants with a historical methodology in which they reproduce and propagate divine truths to bring about personal, social, and political change.

Organization of the Study

Expository preachers attempt to uncover the original meaning of the text based on the original culture and context. There is an underlying assumption that the text is describing a historical situation, which reveals all truth about God or addresses problems in current culture from a divine perspective. Next, the expositor formulates a sermon to identify and address similar problems in contemporary culture and to use the text for speaking to that problem and incorporating modern analogies and illustrations to clarify the points or ideas expressed within the sermon.

According to the SB, an underpinning or foundation of expository preaching is the theological belief that the process for it is methodology and intrinsically sound. SB theologians assert that Biblical Scriptures encompasses divine communication from God as the creator of the universe and all mankind. SB theologians emphasize the importance of studying the Bible as written in the Scriptures's original languages in order to accurately replicate the original culture within the receiving culture. By doing so, the expositor gains assurance about communicating the exact words of God from the original to congregants and listeners.

This self-assurance has empowered the SB theologians and pastors to believe that they are instruments of God who communicate God's objective truth to their congregants and the world at large. SBC entities and congregants share the belief of being stewards of the divine truth that God desires for all people to hear, believe, and follow. Therefore, SB theologians are adamant in their exposition of Scripture and unyielding in their efforts to uphold the traditional, historical, and conservative values they believe to be embedded in scriptural texts. The belief in the expository methodology has emboldened the SBC to actively attempt to influence culture and politics.

Chapter 2 Overview

Chapter 2 demonstrates the historical development of the expository method and shows how SB envision their approach as being based on divine origin. It is a methodology that God and the Bible itself instructs and models. Also, the SBC point to scriptural characters, prophets, apostles, and Jesus Christ as practitioners of expository preaching. Accordingly, SBCs believe that the onus lies with SB pastors and theologians to emulate the expository methodology and to inform its congregants that they are actually communicating the exact words of God. Furthermore, this chapter not only shows the SBC's divine and biblical basis for expository preaching but also demonstrates how this methodology was developed based on an implicit connection to a strong fidelity or belief in the literal translation of the original languages of the biblical text. Additionally, this chapter contains what impels SB expository practitioners to believe that they use scriptural translations and versions that reflect or convey the precise or original scriptural texts.

The influence and successes of expository preaching were seen especially in the twentieth-century when the SB congregants were increasingly influential in affecting national politics and societal values through their adherence to a bibliocentric approach to hermeneutics. The SBC grew to be the largest Protestant denomination in the twentieth century in the United States in part due to its focus on personal evangelism, expository and evangelistic preaching, and its propagation of and adherence to socially conservative values.[2] It typically has been examined as a conservative theological denomination in relation to its conflicts with liberal denominations. However, it is my assertion its belief in and practice of expository preaching enabled SBC to influence not only its own congregants but also other denominational leaders and pastors to accept certain conservative social, economic, and political values.

The growth of the denomination was achieved through a dual pursuit of a fundamental approach to homiletics and a desire to have a preeminent voice in national culture and politics. SBC pastors and theologians are committed to expository preaching and an inherent desire to communicate to their congregants some level of divine communication. The SBC believes that the practice of expository preaching leads to mobilizing congregants to support or negate certain social and political values both financially and personally.

Additionally, this study shows that scriptural texts and expositions, when enshrined in a methodology that assumes inerrancy and inspiration,

---

2. National Council of Churches, "Yearbook."

can lead to an intense sense of polity, loyalty, and personal sacrifice. The examination of this topic includes evidence of how SBC congregations and seminaries possess an undying loyalty to expository preaching and fidelitous translation practices. The narrative shows that SBC congregations and seminaries tend to be consistently dogmatic about a traditional, historic doctrine which SB leaders believe leads to continued congregational growth and development. The SBC's commitment to expository preaching is the foremost methodology which they use to publicly decry, or satiate, certain political or cultural practices. The SBC can claim to do so based on an objective or divine standard that is not based on personal, charismatic, or subjective beliefs. In essence, because the SBC is a "people of the book" and claims to teach the exact meaning of the Bible, the SB theologians and pastors tend to argue that SBC stances are not personal or political but divinely mandated, without bias, for the betterment of the nation and the appeasement of God.

I attempt to show that SB scholarship reacted against the rise of sociological and psychological modes of understanding the world and instead emphasized a mode of interpretation that re-presented the actual truths of the Scripture without any dilution or distortion or engagement in a purely sociological or psychological presenting of the scriptural texts. Their stance was uniquely based on a methodology of interpreting or exegetical study of the original. Conservative theologians also argued that the Bible itself endorses a literal interpretation of Scripture and that the sermon should be based on a literal interpretation of the text. This emphasis on the dual alignment of text and preaching continued to be propagated in the SBC seminaries and encouraged in the pulpit.

In Chapter 2, I demonstrate that the SBC's tendency to assert that they were teaching truth based on the traditional biblical interpretation model, this appealed to the more historically conservative or fundamental religious adherents in American society. Their contention that they teach a historically accurate message from the Bible appeals to congregants who had a historical family connection or shared social values with the SBC. The Southern States especially tend to be more socially, traditionally biblical conservative and more likely to follow traditional values such as prolife, segregation, anti-homosexual, antigambling, and abstinence. These traditional values emerged from historical first-century interpretations of biblical text. However, as in the case of segregation and even gambling, the SBC stances could be considered invented traditions because of their textually questionable hermeneutics and erroneous homiletic applications that might have been based on the cultural preferences of society in the eighteenth and nineteenth centuries.[3]

---

3. Hobswabm and Ranger, *Invention of Tradition*, 2–6.

Chapter 3 Overview

Chapter 3 contains the details of the uniqueness of the SBC and its use of expository preaching. The SBC has articulated its message to attract all Americans, not just Southerners, to its wholeheartedly conservative and dogmatic values. The SBC claims the message has origins in the scriptural text and is not man made. The SBC reports basing these convictions on naturally intrinsic human conscientiousness that correspond with Scripture.

Chapter 3 demonstrates the effectiveness and connection between preaching and personal ideology. The SBC preachers share a message that is consistently traditional and historically conservative. Many non-members share many of the same social, political, and cultural values. Consequently, SBC preaching is not just attractive on a religious level but also on a purely social and political level. Congregants are encouraged to adopt the tenets of SBC preaching so both SBC members and non-members may share similar values because they are expressed communally and oftentimes lead to a sense of community and connectivity.

The third chapter examines the approach of the SBC to ensure that sermons were framed using a translation philosophy which focused on expressing the original meaning of the text. The SBC wanted to ensure that pastors and theologians studied the original languages or used a Bible translation or version that was close to the original. The New American Standard Bible (NASB) became one of the preferred versions, and another favored Bible version was the New King James Version (NKJV), as it too followed the literal method of translation. Both versions were considered a "complete equivalence" as against a "dynamic equivalence."[4] I demonstrate that the SB pastors and theologians who focus on these and other specific versions of the Bible ensure that their exegetical model represents accurate rendering of the original text.

The hermeneutical principles or language rules for genre analysis constructed specific views about pertinent cultural and political areas such as the role of government, wealth and materialism, the family, the existence and prevalence of good and evil, entertainment, and the eschatological role of the United States. There is a duality in this process that reflects certain social and cultural values. However, the expository methodology, according to the SB theologians, produces or reveals these views as embedded in the biblical text. Therefore, SBC pastors and theologians are convinced of the biblical accuracy of their messages, even though their messages likely reflect the secular conservatism of the congregants and even non-members. The SB

---

4. Nida, "Toward a Science of Translating."

theologians's views or beliefs emerge naturally from scriptural text as part of the process of expository preaching, namely exegesis and hermeneutics.

The dominant translation theory of SB theologians argued for fidelity rather than freedom in the exchange of source and receptor languages, aiming for the accurate dissemination of texts of the Scripture. The idea of fidelity for the SBC theologians is a word-for-word transmission of the message from the source text written in Hebrew, Aramaic, or Greek. Fidelity includes maintaining the syntax and grammar of the source text. This translation model passes on the message of the original in both sense and form and produces the same effect of the original text to the receptor culture. SBC theologians assert that a divine impact happens to contemporary hearers when they receive the same message as the original hearers. The underlying assertion is that the "very words of God" are conserved and conveyed, which is effective in bringing about personal transformation.

Chapter 3 contains an analysis of the methodology of exegesis (including genre analysis) as practiced and endorsed by the foremost SBC theologians, leaders, and pastors. I describe the relationship between the exegetical and hermeneutic methodology that perpetuates SBC ideologies, as well as SBC social and political views. I anthologize the accounts of preachers and interpreters regarding their practices. Some of the central figures's writings that are discussed include Daniel Akin (president of Southeastern Seminary), David Allen (Professor of Theology and Homiletics at Southwestern Seminary), Jim Shaddix (Professor of Preaching at Southeastern Seminary), R. Albert Mohler, Jr. (President of Southern Baptist Theological Seminary; Joseph Emerson Brown (Professor of Christian Theology). These individuals have served in SBC pulpits, on SBC higher education faculties, and well as in leadership roles in SBC seminaries. I examine their writings, sermons, and conduct interviews regarding their homiletic methodology.

I explain that the conceptual framework that this group of theologians have used to interpret the Scriptures is encompassed in a spiral movement from the original text and audience in its original meaning to its contemporization or acculturation in the twentieth century.[5] Expository preaching involves studying the text in the original language by using proven linguistic and scientific methods. The language of the text is structured or organized in a communicable and palpable manner homiletically by using proven communication techniques in an attempt to convey the meaning of the text. These SB theologians and pastors share a mutual commitment to expository preaching and maintain the same theological beliefs in which they emphasize their respective leadership roles to influence congregations, seminaries,

---

5. This interpretative methodology is detailed in Osborne, *Hermeneutical Spiral*.

and other SBC entities. They express a similar, conservative belief system that involves a commitment to the process of expository preaching. Furthermore, through an analysis of the foremost hermeneutic and homiletic textbooks used in SBC seminaries, I demonstrate their practice of depending on a belief in this conceptual framework. Important to the spiral movement through the process of exegesis and hermeneutics is genre analysis used to determine the genre or type of literature in which a passage or text is found.

Chapter 4 Overview

In chapter 4, I focus on SBC translation methodology that supports the SB theologians's need for purity and literalness in understanding the Bible as written in the original Hebrew, Aramaic, and Greek. SBC theologians and pastors have long asserted that many other denominations or cultic groups find their beginnings through the erroneous understanding of the text or because of mistranslations. They argue that historically many churches, congregations or denominations establish their belief system and certain theological beliefs without adequately studying the actual scriptural text or without even attempting to understand the actual meaning of the original. Instead, they assert that many readers of the Bible make decisions based on the English translation without studying the overall semantic and linguistic structure of the text. They point to the Reformation and the theologically faulty practices of the Roman Catholic Church and the laity's lack of Bible reading or just accessibility to the Bible. The SBC has always advocated for the priesthood of believers that enables individual congregants to have access to an accurate or literal rendering of the original text and ensuring congregants hear sermons that are based on biblical translations that are as close to the original as possible or as literal a rendering as possible of the original.

In an effort to maintain certain foundational biblical ideals, the SB theologians support a translation principle based on fidelity or formal equivalence rather than functional or dynamic equivalence. Functional equivalence translations such as New Living Translation (NLT) and the New Century Version (NCV) are used to as mere reference points in the homiletic process. They are oftentimes alluded to for highlighting an idea or thought, needing to express an idea in a culturally savvy or relevant manner, and showing how a word or phrase can be stated in a different, but understandable manner. The NLT and NCV are never used by SB theologians and pastors as the main translations for conveying biblical meaning during preaching.

SB theologians are concerned with translating the original text word for word and ensuring the replication of the lexical and syntactical structure of the original biblical presentation. The standard texts used in SBC churches serve to support and maintain the traditional, historical biblical values related to critical societal and cultural issues, such as the complementarian roles of men and women in the church and society. The SBC has avowed the complementarian roles of men and women, namely the idea that women live in a functionally subordinate role in marriage and church leadership, though equal in essence to men. The idea of submission to a man in marriage and only men as the pastors and major leaders in the church has been propagated through expository preaching and teaching.

The SBC's translation process has proliferated the patriarchal view of the Old Testament Bible and advocated for the male leadership views of the New Testament. The SBC exposits that the gender-neutral or egalitarian views of men and women are not biblical. Their schema of expository preaching emphasizes a hierarchy in which all marriages, not just Christian marriages, males exercise the right of leadership and hold the final say in all decisions and plans in their families. Additionally, SBC pastors are men, and Christian males have the final say in all decisions regarding the operations of each SBC church. The primary teaching responsibility during the weekend services belongs to men. The SBC's literal translation principle has not only yielded literal renderings of the original biblical texts but also has irrevocably shaped and supported the language and culture of the Bible to reiterate SBC biblical theology about gender roles, human sexuality, and other gender issues important to the political and social arena in the United States.

Chapter 5 Overview

In the final chapter, Chapter 5, I describe the social and political views that emanate from engaging in expository preaching. I note how the sermons from various pulpits influence political establishments based on the theological stances presented in SB expositors's preaching. I show that the expository method was a potent methodology for affecting social and political change and for galvanizing the polity for social, cultural, and political causes. In order to demonstrate their social and political influence, I review opinion polls, newspaper articles, listenership, and viewership of SBC radio and TV broadcasts, politicians affiliated with the SBC and their voting records and laws supported or enacted, funding for lobby-groups and their resultant effectiveness, church attendance records and their commercial enterprises and publications. I argue that the use of expository preaching garnered widespread appeal because it had a sacrosanct association with objective truth. Therefore, the social issues supported by the SBC warranted a hermeneutical and homiletic model that supposedly maintained the veracity of their beliefs. SBC pastors and leaders have used their pulpits and the expository form of preaching as a vanguard for motivating and inspiring their congregants to act in accordance with the underlying biblical ideas that express God's will. SBC pastors also demand obedience from their congregants to ensure that society and culture are not corrupted.

By examining the role of expository preaching and its innate characteristics and its espousal by the SBC in the twentieth-century, I demonstrate the influence of an exegetical, hermeneutic, and translation methodology in not only increasing or building a denomination but also affecting social and political change. I examine records addressing the ideological and political conflicts in the SBC to show how the SBC's approaches to their social values impact national and social arenas.

Significance of the Study

This project provides literary scholars and theologians with a better understanding of some practices to utilize or avoid in developing hermeneutical and homiletic theory. Additionally, this examination includes a focus on the historical development and use of expository preaching by SB pastors and its misapplications which hinder the growth of the SBC. Furthermore, the belief in the principles and practice of expository preaching by SB pastors contributed to the controversial and significant conservative resurgence. This resurgence resulted in the removal of several important theologians from leadership positions and employment in SB seminaries, publications, and other educational entities. Expository preaching influenced the SBC approach to social and political values, and I show that religious texts do not function in isolation but are used to transmit certain social and political values because denominations rely on a complex and strategic interrelationship among theologians, pastors, religious leaders, and denominational seminaries and institutions of higher learning. The commitment to expository preaching resulted in the literal reading, interpretation, and application of the scriptural text to the extent that congregants were mobilized to influence electoral candidates, support or boycott certain corporations, and discriminate against certain groups of people.

What is intriguing about the approach of the SBC involves how their doctrines and beliefs claimed to have stemmed from careful, exegetical study as part of understanding the meaning of the original text. The results or doctrinal beliefs that emanate from their efforts are held and preached with strong commitment. However, SBC leaders simultaneously maintain an understanding that these are not social or cultural principles but divine oracles which transcend culture and time. SB theologians and pastors claim that they cannot take responsibility for the doctrines and beliefs from which the expository was derived due to the exegetical and homiletic approach. They claim their belief system is corroborated by biblical writers, ancient practitioners of exposition, patristic theologians, and even the Reformers.

Chapter 2

Historical Development of Expository Preaching

CHAPTER 2 FOCUSES ON the historical development of expository preaching and the various facets which comprise the discipline and a review the SBC's historical basis for practicing expository preaching. The practice of expository preaching is founded on the hermeneutical principles espoused from early first century Christians through twentieth-century Christians. Essentially, SBC theologians studied the different hermeneutic and homiletic models practiced during the early years of Christianity and accepted the model which received widespread acceptance from the more conservative church fathers and theologians. SB theologians, pastors, and leaders demonstrate its advocacy when formulating the SBC biblical theology and social agenda. I examine historical sermons as well as theological and homiletic works. I consider biographical data of some of the foremost SBC expositors, historians, and theologians who include John Leadley Dagg, A. T. Robertson, John A. Broadus, W. A. Criswell, and Paige Patterson.

Theological and Scriptural Veracity

Expository preaching is based on an implicit belief that the Scriptural text is truthful. Also, the belief is that behind the written text, a real cosmic conflict rooted in human history not only gives rise to the original written Scripture but also accounts for the urgency and importance of expositing the literal meaning of these texts and teaching the entirety of the Bible. This cosmic conflict motif can be eschatologically realized only at the end of human history. In order to satisfy the demands of the divine God, SB expositors believe in telling congregants about the creation of human history, which began with the rebellion of the angelic being, Satan, and his banishment with a host of demonic angelic beings (Satan's followers who also rebelled against God) to an uncreated earth. Satan sought to thwart God's plans for human creation.

Satan successfully tempted the first human beings and plunged humanity into a state of fallenness or sin that results in an immediate, personal separation from God. Beginning with the book of Genesis, the Bible recounts God's creation, punishment, and atonement of sin. The biblical texts tell the stories of the ancient patriarchs, the nation of Israel, and the advent of Jesus Christ and his apostles. SB theologians point to the very beginnings in Genesis as the historical starting point of understanding God's purpose for individuals, marriage, family, and society. No specific biblical commands stipulate that the text should be read and interpreted sequentially; however, it is important to note that some of the fundamental SBC ideals find their foundational support in the text of Genesis. SBC theologians and pastors argue that the lives of the biblical characters represent how God wants people to live in order to please him and not experience divine punishment like that experienced by Satan and the other fallen angels.

According to the SB pastors and theologians, the scriptural text is an accurate record of human history through the eyes of God and its preservation and transmission teaches human beings how to relate to and please God. Failure to please God and meet his divine standards results in divine punishment and judgement. SB theologians and pastors subscribe to the belief that the Bible is a special revelation and a direct communication or special revelation from God to the prophets, scribes, and writers. It is God's communication to men. Biblical texts were spoken to men in words, which they wrote to preserve God's messages and ensure those messages could be transmitted and taught to all people.

Additionally, for SB theologians and pastors, the Scripture is true and applicable for all ages throughout human history. The Bible facilitates the reconciliation between God and humankind. It is absolutely critical that the original meaning and original intent of the Bible writers is revealed so that men and women hear and understand God's words. The ultimate goal of SB preaching is to gain faith in and obedience to God and to avoid God's wrath, punishment, and judgment.

SB believe that it is only the texts of Scripture, God's special revelation that can result in faith and cause human beings to please God and avoid his wrath and judgment. There are two aspects to the working or birthing of faith according to SB the third person of the Trinity, the Holy Spirit, divinely uses the text to bring about personal conviction and repentance. The Holy Spirit's work is predicated on the accurate dissemination of the text because the Holy Spirit only (based on SB theology) works based on the original truths of the text. SB pastors and theologians are engrossed with the concept of expositing the tenets of Scripture because they believe that God will not empower congregants to believe mistranslations or inaccurate teachings. SB pastors and theologians believe in piety and personal success, meaning that an individual's success is determined based on obedience and belief in biblical text. Therefore, when pastors or theologians fail to exposit the truth and teach erroneous doctrines, they not only risk personal punishment but also can cause congregants not to experience personal success from God. This success may include material wealth, good health, a prolific life-style of personal evangelism, generosity and being generally well-liked by congregants and non-members.

Essentially, hearing the original text with its authentic original commands and decrees, believing and following them, causes listeners to experience the power of God. Many SB and other theologians affirm the divinity of unadulterated scriptural text and promote expositions free of erroneous mistakes. Exposition must be imparted and permeated with God's power. In other words, believing and obeying results in unusual, unexplained, or enabling power and strength. Theologian Wayne Grudem recognizes the Bible as God's communication in written form as a special revelation to human beings and as the personal embodiment and expression of the mind of Jesus Christ. Grudem attaches value and significance to the Bible because of its innate divine characteristics.[1] Consequently, the Bible constitutes the tangible manifestation of God's purposes and designs for biblical adherents.

Historically, then the SB pastors and theologians believe that expository preaching is absolutely necessary because of the personal benefits to both the expositor and congregants as well as because of the personal consequences of not living according to the tenets of the scriptural texts. Furthermore, SB theologians and pastors believe in the exclusivity of the Gospel and no other text than the Bible offers a means to know and experience God and Jesus Christ. However, in order to be a member of a SB church the congregant must attest to a unique perspective about Jesus, be willing to emulate Jesus, and be personally baptized. SB theologians and pastors believe in a literal interpretation of the biblical text that includes literal teachings about and by Jesus and other Bible writers are expected to be practiced or followed. This view is foundational to understanding expository preaching

---

1. Grudem, *Systematic Theology*, 47–50.

because the Bible in its literal form is truthful or accurate, and by practicing the lessons of the Bible, a congregant literally can attain personal appeasement of God, personal experience and knowledge of God, and ultimately at the end of the cosmic conflict, an eternal state with God. SB theologians and pastors also argue that only through encountering the literal, accurate renderings of the Bible through expository preaching, teaching, or literal translating do people gain an authentic, personal knowledge and experience of God's power and become aware of his presence in their lives. SB argue that the Bible is the only power, the only modality, the only cause and source to know God and Jesus, and to experience the Triune aspects of God.

SB theologians and pastors assert that the Bible is the only gateway to personally experiencing God. As a gateway, the Bible must be accurately disseminated or else the biblical encounter through preaching is false and ineffectual. They believe that through commitment to the church may one believe in living according to God's standards, experiencing relative material prosperity, and enjoying a stable family environment. However, SB theologians and pastors firmly believe that following doctrines antithetical to SB beliefs, especially in the area of personal salvation and spiritual growth, creates a situation that can lead the individual to face eternal judgment based on wrong beliefs and practices. In essence, SB theologians and pastors believe that earthly success is uncertain because of the certainty that is only obtainable in the final judgement.

Additionally, individual SB followers may feel a personal conviction about being saved. However, faith is so deeply personal and private, there are times when even signs do not reveal motives or the true intent of an individual's heart. Thus, SB theologians experience tension with the likelihood of some individuals claiming to be adherents when they are not. Accordingly, even though there are signs in people's behaviors indicating true faith, ultimately the real authentication of one's personal salvation comes at the eschatological end of time. The exposition of scriptural text through the process of exegesis, hermeneutics, and homiletics is paramount to gleaning the original meaning so that congregants can experience and know the power of God. The foundational concept to expository preaching which warrants SBC support and belief in the methodology begins with the idea that God has spoken to human beings and his words are powerful for life and salvation. Consequently, congregants must hear the original, authentic, and literal tenets of the scriptural texts.

L. S. Chafer, founder of Dallas Theological Seminary, emphasized the indispensable value of the Scripture:

> No substitute will ever be found for the knowledge of the Word of God. That Word alone deals with things eternal and infinite, and it alone has the power to convert the soul and to develop a God-honoring spiritual life. There is a limitless, yet hidden, spiritual content within the Bible which contributes much to its supernatural character.[2]

Conservative theologian Charles Hodge argues for the veracity of the scriptural texts.[3] However, it becomes apparent that the SBC is caught in a circularity argument for the basis of their belief is derived from the very text about which they advocate. They assert that the Bible is true and powerful because the Bible says it is true and powerful. This biblical self-determinacy wherein theologians and pastors base their assertion about the Bible from the Bible seems somewhat illogical. Nonetheless, the SBC theologians argue that the personal testimony of congregants that include their authentic experiences of the presence and power of God in various circumstances of life provide evidence for the divinity of the Bible. SB pastors sometimes point to miraculous experiences, whereby the very thing for which they pray comes to fruition and the sense of tranquility in the face of the danger or trouble overcomes them because of their confidence that God is with them in the present.

SB theologians, pastors, and congregants use personal testimonies to counter the circular argument even though it is accepted and understood that the Bible is the sole authority. However, they use personal testimonies to present proof that their methodology actually works in the lives of people. It is undoubtedly difficult to argue with one's personal testimony especially if its results can be corroborated in the case when a difficult circumstance was removed or solved through intercession and prayers. There are many non-congregants who are responsible for conglomerates, corporations, world leaders, national leaders, business leaders or professionals who resolve insurmountable problems who thrive in the midst of difficulty and who experience personal prosperity without a commitment to or following a specific biblical text. There is an apparent dichotomy and unresolved tension for congregants and non-congregants have the same life experiences and both sometimes make legally appropriate decisions or fail to uphold legal and ethical standards. Congregants also can never consistently obey every tenet of the text in all of life's daily circumstances for it is almost impossible to know the entirety of the scriptural text and so know which text to apply in every given situation. If power comes through hearing and appropriation

2. Chafer, *Systematic Theology*, vi.
3. Hodge, *Systematic Theology*, 38.

then congregants are rendered powerless through witlessness, or because of the inaccessibility to expository preaching or even due to insufficient exegesis or exposition of the text. Therein it seems that the expositor has a unfathomable responsibility and the personal failure of the congregant may be due to the expositor's inexperience and as such should remove culpability from the congregant. The act of expository preaching then appears to inherently bear some level of implicit power, the act both conveys divine powerful words and is also responsible for the empowerment of the hearers.

It is noteworthy too that the SBC theologians and pastors affirm that power and empowerment are gained not just through the commands and obedience to propositional scriptural text but also through the understanding and personal application of the principles in the various literary forms. There is a divine revelation to be lived out in the various images, riddles, narratives, poems, and so on. SBC pastors and theologians argue for a system of analyzing different genres because God speaks in various forms, and God's various forms of speech are meant to be believed and obeyed. In other words, expository preaching and its commitment to exegesis by following the rules of semantic and syntactic analysis, grammar, historical, and cultural context makes it possible to discover the original meaning behind an act of God in the scriptural text or a speech in the scriptural text.[4]

Accordingly, expository preaching proponents contend that the act of exegesis and hermeneutics of biblical text and the communication of biblical text through the practice of proper homiletic theory convey principles, propositional ideas, or commands, depending on the genre or nature of the sermon. Through the careful exposition of the scriptural text, the expositor unearths the meaning that God wants to convey to the congregants. That is why SBC theologians and pastors are firmly committed to the process of hermeneutics so that they can assert that regardless of the form or genre, event or circumstances that led to the recording of a biblical text its intended meaning has been uncovered. The expository process serves as proof to themselves that they have revealed the divine intended meaning and are conveying a divine message to the congregants. This divine message should be proclaimed and upheld at all cost. Furthermore, due to its divine nature, the message has eschatological implications for culture. The text's nonapplication hastens divine judgment of eschatological events, such as natural disasters or theological tribulation. The message or command should be adopted and practiced by all of the culture even if it means solicitation of political support. In other words according to SB doctrine, the text provides directives for personal action, and when personal action is insufficient to

---

4. Alexander and Rosner, *New Dictionary of Biblical Theology*.

accomplish those directives, adherents must turn to political means to ensure the application of the text.

Accordingly, the conceptual framework of expository preaching is predicated on the concept of the innate power that is in the words of the scriptural text regardless of the event or circumstance or genre that precipitated the recording of the event. Also, SB theologians and pastors regard the Scripture as divine communication from God and the pastor, teacher, or theologians as the stewards and messengers of divine communication. A failure to maintain the accuracy of the original is considered heretical and may lead to divine angst and judgment as against those who misinterpret the Bible. This is the argument of the SBC who conceive from their own exposition scriptural text.[5]

It becomes problematic however as there is no measurable standard for determining if an expositor has unearthed all the salient commands or ideas in a given text, word or sentence. Also, there is no way to determine the transformative effect of a text. It seems that congregational growth and attendance are the only reflections of the impact of the message or its powerful, transformative effect in the lives of its listeners. SB tend to equate powerful sermons and effective preaching with congregational growth and tend to highlight skilled oratorical expositors as good models for expository preaching. In other words, SBC considers its large churches and their pastors as effective models of expositional preaching and as exceptional leaders to be emulated even though some of their sermons may not meet the demands of good exegesis and homiletics. Also, there are pastors who do careful exegesis but their delivery or homiletics is tedious or uninteresting even though they have unearthed the divine message or truth. Consequently, their congregants are deterred or distracted from listening to the message.

The SBC contends that the transformative power of the biblical text only comes into effect after the experience of salvation followed by ongoing listening, believing, and practicing of the tenets of the biblical text. By ongoing engagement, personal transformation or sanctification is empowered by the Holy Spirit, the Pnuema acting on the scriptural texts. The scriptural texts, particularly the "speech-acts," are the modes used by the expositors to develop sermons that contain evidence of the practicality of following the mandates of the texts. There is another hermeneutical element, as there are moments in a text, which illustrate the character's stream of consciousness and does not merit an exegetical or homiletic proposition to which congregants must conform. This is where the expositor decides what descriptive of

---

5. Dr. W. A. Criswell, foremost SBC expositor, commented during his expository sermon on Rev 22:18–19, preached on September 29, 1963, about the judgment of God on any individual that misuses, misinterprets or alters the Biblical text.

that time and culture is applied; however, it is not prescriptive as an act to bring about sanctification and the congregant's obedience.

SB expositors, theologians, and pastors have long held to the doctrine of inspiration and inerrancy. The concept of inspiration functions as the basis for assuming what scriptural texts are prescriptive and are necessary for the salvation and sanctification process. Inerrancy, then represents the foundation for the expository performance of preaching. The expositor, through the belief in inerrancy, asserts that the translated scriptural texts are true or accurate to the original autographs and manuscripts from which the translated original biblical text emerged. Thus, the expositor assumes that the human speech that is recorded as scriptural text has been written as God instructed the biblical writers and that they wrote exactly what God told them to write. Even some of their prophetic acts or the behavior of the prophets and biblical writers, their deeds and words said to the nation of Israel, surrounding nations, or the early church are in some cases necessary for the experience of salvation and sanctification and in other cases it reveals God's perspective about people though that too comes with implicit divine expectations.

SB pastors and theologians then rely on the concept of inspiration and inerrancy as the groundwork for substantiating the authority, authenticity, and sanctify purpose of the Scriptures and the necessity then for the expository to meticulous engage in the exegetical and homiletic process of expository preaching. Furthermore, the SBC understands Scripture in which the texts of Scripture are interpreted as verbally and plenary inspired. Essentially, SB theologians and pastors believe that the Bible is authored by both God and man in that God worked through the Scripture writers to ensure that the final product represents the very words that God wanted to communicate. This logic sounds much like a mechanical exchange between God and man this concept of inspiration, but the SBC believes that God so directed all human authors to write without suspending their own personalities and idiosyncrasies, even while maintaining the veracity of God's communication.

A commendable approach by the SBC involves believing that every text in the Bible is as God intended and that biblical writers wrote according to their own stylistic preferences. According to SB pastors and theologians, biblical writers experienced God as comprehensively working in their lives to ensure what they wrote appears without any error or mistake. Biblical writers experienced the sanctifying agent of God to the extent that they were under God's full and complete control, even though they also still controlled their faculties in a perfectly faultless state. The SBC believes that this combination of the God-man partnership in producing biblical text is necessary for salvation and sanctification. The God-man partnership does represent the ideal soteriological relationship but does underscore the relative difficulty in congregational sanctification as the experience of canonization appears sporadic, incomplete, and obstructed. The expository preaching act does not guarantee a divine connection in the preaching moment between God and the congregant yet allows for the dissemination of the truth with sheer oratory skill to attract attendees. However, the scope of the expository sermon foresees congregants making life changes to reflect the doctrine of these SBC beliefs and practices.

The other theological pillar that SB theologians and pastors rely on is the concept of inerrancy and its related doctrine of infallibility. The process of contextualizing the text as a part of the homiletic methodology involves ensuring that the original intent or meaning is maintained. The interpreter or expositor exclusively committed to the theological doctrine of the Bible and to the doctrines of inspiration and inerrancy becomes obligated thereafter to follow the methodology that ensures the expositor garners the original meaning of the text. From there, the expositor expounds the meaning whilst maintaining the relevance of the text when preaching to contemporary hearers. One of the arguments put forth by the SBC regarding the reliability of the biblical text is the subjective, but non-measurable, notion of personal witness. The SBC points to the concept of canonicity, which is the selection, consolidation, and historical affirmation of the Bible's sixty-six books.

In a Christian context, the word "canon" refers to "the list of the writings acknowledged by the Church as documents of divine revelation." Athanasius, bishop of Alexandria, used the word in this sense in a letter circulated in AD 367.[6] The word does not simply denote a list of works, but canon was used to represent the "rule of faith" or "rule of truth." Indeed, in the early Christian centuries, the scriptural texts were considered a standard for belief and practice of the Christian faith. Athanasius drew on the work of Origen in 367 enumerated Christian documents considered to be canonical, and with miniscule changes, his lists and Origen reflected the current sixty-six books of the Reformation Bible. Athanasius made a distinction between the scriptural texts and those that could be used for inspiration and edification.[7] Hence, a more fundamental methodology for asserting the reliability of the scriptural text rather than purely referring to inerrancy and inspiration is the historical criterion.

---

6. Hanson, *Origen's Doctrine of Tradition*, 71, 78, 79, 208.
7. Bruce, *Canon of Scripture*, 77.

The scriptural text themselves could be said to be integral to the church and polity because of its role in antiquity. Early Christian theologians believed that a literary work was canonical if it represented an apostle's work or the work of someone closely associated with an apostle and was written during the apostolic age. Any narrative or epistolary letter written later than the apostolic age could not be included in the canonical books. The scriptural text themselves have authoritative force because of their historical roots and acceptance by the ancient theological tyros of the early Christian church. These texts were based on the original or beginning Christian faith's standard or rule of practice, which makes the scriptural text that fits this criterion, specifically the New Testament text, a controlling force for converts. Furthermore, the concept of orthodoxy does seem more relevant as the framework for utilizing the biblical text as the source of belief and practice with the assumption that it can be used for salvation and sanctification. Orthodoxy, conveys the idea that the scriptural text fits within a constancy or common theological grid, that means the scriptural text can be assumed to be authoritative for a specific denomination such as the SBC because the congregation was founded on the rule or standard of the biblical text and follows the same pattern of belief that is theologically consistent to biblical text in what they advocate and disavow.

The power for transformation through the "speech-acts" of the scriptural text which has been presented to the polity through the exposition of the text relies on the unearthing of the original meaning and being orated homiletically. However, the power that the SBC alludes to in the text operates as a possible source in its appeal to its apostolicity and orthodoxy and even to its widespread acceptance and use by the evangelical church at large (i.e., the Roman Catholic and Protestant churches). The sixty-six books of the Old and New Testament have been universally recognized by the evangelical church to be the standard for belief and practice. Therefore, congregants, without needing to know their church history, are aware that at least for generations their churches have used a Bible with sixty-six books to authenticate their faith, to regulate their practice, and to appeal to it as the means for salvation and sanctification, and to allude to it as the standard for mobilizing behavior in society and culture.

The SB idea of inspiration when connected with the concepts of apostolicity, orthodoxy, historicity or antiquity, and catholicity provides credence for the transformative role of the Bible's texts. The Bible plays a controlling role in their faith community because of its historical attestation and role in the community which has been passed down from generations. Also, when combined with the consistent referencing and quoting of the Bible during moments of expository preaching or when citing theological dogma as authoritative, inerrant, and inspired this constructs a creedal understanding of the nature and role of the Bible. A cursory survey, of Old Testament text such as Psalm 19:7–10 discusses the supremacy of the Bible:

> The law of the Lord is perfect, restoring the soul; the testimony of the LORD is sure, making wise the simple. The precepts of the LORD are right, rejoicing the heart; the commandment of the LORD is pure, enlightening the eyes. The fear of the LORD is clean, enduring forever; the judgments of the LORD are true; they are righteous altogether. They are more desirable than gold, yes, than much fine gold; Sweeter also than honey and the drippings of the honeycomb.

Deuteronomy 11:18–20 too expresses the value of the Scriptures,

> You shall therefore impress these words of mine on your heart and on your soul; and you shall bind them as a sign on your hand, and they shall be as frontals on your forehead. You shall teach them to your sons, talking of them when you sit in your house and when you walk along the road and when you lie down and when you rise up. You shall write them on the doorposts of your house and on your gates.

These verses from Psalms and Deuteronomy demonstrate the conventional, internal attestation as to the veracity and transformative purpose of the scriptural text which SBC theologians and pastors fully support. The exegetical process of examining the Hebrew text indicates both a structure and form which supports the meaning of the text. This passage is the embodiment of a linguistic speech-act, but one which is verifiable by the exegetical analysis that reveals its meaning. Also, the text is canonical, corroborated by its antiquity and consistency with evangelical orthodoxy. The challenge for SB theologians is to anchor their exposition using verifiable historical analysis in substantiation of the reading or the original text. This effort would present a delineation in their methodology; however, it would corroborate their understanding of originality, inerrancy, and inspiration.

The Theological Role of the Old Testament Prophet

Historically, the SBC pastor has recognized his role as following the ancient and biblical path of the prophet. He saw himself as not only responsible for proclaiming the original intent of the author but also to present it to the congregation in an understandable and relevant manner. Their role was an extension of the Old Testament prophetic role. In that they were forth-telling, reporting of things as they were and how they should be from a divine perspective. The other aspect of the Old Testament prophetic office is that of fore-telling, speaking about future events from a divine perspective. Based on the Old Testament Law, the Old Testament prophet should face death if his forth-telling was in contradiction with the Law and if his foretelling of events did not come to pass. In other words, the Old Testament prophet should be a repository of truth. His message and his office or role were dependent on the consistency of his message with the Old Testament Law and the substantiation of his prophecy.

The SBC pastors and theologians recognize this tremendous responsibility as the mouthpiece or messenger of God. Congregants like the people of the Old Testament expect that their pastors and theologians are functioning in a manner emblematic a messenger of God. SBC pastors's and theologians's messages must be accurate and true. They should be prepared, and what they communicate must be in tandem with the divine prerogative. The effectiveness of expository preaching especially in the SBC seminaries is based on the concept of the expositor as a messenger, a mouthpiece of God.

Moreover, SBC pastors and theologians understand their message to be wholly inerrant as did the prophets of antiquity. This understanding, in a sense, supports their work of exegesis and homiletics in communicating the original message from the divine. The authority of the message is primarily internally based, but there are external indicators as well. Also, the overall canonicity of the text enshrouds the message with a level of authority. The authoritative and transformative self-witness of the text along with the personal witness of the polity gives credence to scriptural text. There is a seemingly dualistic belief in both the authority of the preacher and the text.

The SB expositor proclaims the orthodox, catholic text from antiquity to be authoritative and inspired. By this exposition, the SBC pastor receives recognition as credible or ethical because of the task of expository preaching and his inherent prophetic character is accepted as ethically credible based on the cultic office he represents. The SB expositor through the tasks of exegesis and homiletics bridges the cultural and linguistic gaps between the original text and the receptor culture. Furthermore, because of his prophetic role, he must ensure to disseminate the text accurately using the original meaning of the Scripture so that congregants may hear and respond to the divine message. It seems that much more is expected of the expositor than the individual congregant. Due the eschatological dimension of the exposition and its problematic possibility of judgment and rewards for congregants based on their religious practice, the expositor's role receives high esteem while the sacerdotal task of expositional preaching is vital to state of mind and perspective of the polity.

In the Old Testament, the primary means for communicating or preaching the word of God was through the אִיבָנ (*nābî*), or spokesman and prophet from the verb *nāba*, and literally this word means "to call," "to proclaim," and hence, "to pour forth words, like those who speak with fervor of mind or under divine inspiration, as prophets and poets."[8] The prophet shared or proclaimed discourse from God through God's Spirit. The prophet was acutely aware of his intermediary role as God's spokesperson his primary responsibility was that of representing God before man and not necessarily in a priestly function of representing man before God. Whereas the Old Testament priest engaged in the service of the sacrificial cultic ceremony of worship, the prophet specifically communicated an undiluted divine message.

The importance of the prophetic role of the expositor and his commitment to expository preaching is foundational to SBC pastors and theologians. The SBC and its seminaries have sought to develop expositors and ensure that its seminaries focus on orthodox theological doctrines and in so doing influence its congregants to believe the same especially regarding doctrines regarding the scriptural text and believing the transformative power of the Bible. SBC pastors and theologians have attempted to affirm the inerrancy, infallibility, and inspiration of the scriptural text and the importance and art of expository preaching. SBC pastors and seminary graduates must adhere to SB doctrines and preach expository sermons with the understanding that they can influence their congregations to follow and believe certain theological and social values.

The first SB seminary was founded with the specific purpose of developing SB preachers, pastors, and leaders who hold to orthodox, conservative doctrines, especially those concerning the Bible and to prepare then to become expository preachers. The seminary was established in 1859, in Greenville, South Carolina, where the seminary's founder, James Petigru Boyce, was joined by John A. Broadus, Basil Manly, Jr., and William Williams as the seminary's first faculty. In 1857, J. B. Jeter, a leading SB pastor of the nineteenth century and then pastor of Grace Baptist Church in Richmond, Virginia, described the purpose of Southern Seminary, the oldest of the SBC seminaries, in the following manner:

> Being free from the shackles imposed by the old systems and established precedents, and having all the lights of experience and observation to guide us, we propose to found an institution suited to the genius, wants, and circumstances of our denomination; in which shall be taught with special attention the true

---

8. VanGemeren, *New International Dictionary*, 1067–78.

principles of expounding the Scriptures and the art of preaching efficiently the Gospel of Christ.[9]

Jeter believed that the seminary's main role was the preparation of expositors. The seminary was primarily established to train men on how to exposit the biblical text. Also, on July 30, 1856, James Petigru Boyce delivered his inaugural address of Southern Seminary entitled "Three Changes in Theological Education." Boyce commented as follows:

> In adopting this change we are as far from saying that education is unnecessary that we proclaim its absolute necessity. We undertake, however, to point out what education it is that is thus essential, and what that which is only valuable; and while we urge upon all to acquire all useful knowledge as an aid to that work, *we point out the knowledge of the word of God as that which is first in importance.*[10]

On the celebration of the seventy-fifth anniversary of the seminary, Seminary President John R. Sampey commented on eight ideals and "goals which stir the Seminary to race at top speed." Sampey described the list in the following manner:

> Let me put in the foreground the Seminary's devotion to the Holy Scriptures. The Bible in Hebrew and Greek and English is at the foundation of the entire course of study. Believing that the Scriptures are God-breathed, the Seminary refuses its higher degrees to men who will not learn enough Hebrew and Greek to read the Bible in the original languages. The Scriptures are our sufficient and authoritative rule of faith and practice.[11]

The SBC from its onset was focused and devoted to biblical training in the original languages so that the expositor could convey the original intent and they followed the premise regarding the sufficiency and power of the Scriptures for faith and practice. The attempted to develop conservative students who in turn would lead and influence its congregations to embrace and uphold conservative values. Southern Seminary introduced inventive approaches to seminary education by using the English Bible in teaching biblical courses as opposed to using only Hebrew and Greek texts. Furthermore, they offered a seminary education for individuals studying classes other than the classical disciplines.[12] The seminary sought to attract

---

9. Broadus, *Memoir of James Petigru Boyce*, 148.
10. Boyce, "Three Changes," 25.
11. Shurden, "Southern Seminary," 394.
12. Shurden, "Southern Seminary," 394.

preachers and pastors who had no previous formal religious education as well as students who had theological training but wanted a seminary education. Their ultimate goal was to shape the denominations churches and develop a system for generating a consistent type of pastor and theologian. One that indorses the SB theological doctrines and proclaimed the same to its churches and congregants.

Moreover, John Broadus wrote his classic text on expository preaching, *On The Preparation and Delivery of Sermons*, in 1870, and it became the standard text on preaching in the seminary. This text detailed the properties of expository preaching and popularized the exegetical and homiletic approach that utilized the historical, grammatical, contextual analysis combined with an effective rhetorical but theologically astute style of presentation. Prior to the publication of Broadus's text and the establishment of Southern Seminary, the SBC and its churches were more focused on topical sermons. This prevailing methodology was deductive eisegeses or in some cases proof-texting without examining or using the text in its specific cultural context or without studying the original meaning.

In 1892, E. C. Dargan joined the faculty of Southern Seminary as a professor of homiletics and pastoral theology, his fifteen years of homiletics instruction led to *The History of Preaching*, a two-volume historical study of the craft. Dargan also edited Broadus's classic *Preparation and Delivery of Sermons* and taught a sociology course at the seminary. He credited Broadus with changing the SB approach of preaching of his day from the mere spiritualizing of the sermon to a more expository style of preaching.[13]

W. O. Carver served as Professor of Missions from 1898–1943, though he was not a theological conservative, Dale Moody described him as an evolutionist and "a salty old liberal," who "thought Barth and Brunner were just a bunch of fundamentalists."[14] He claimed that Broadus was instrumental in converting the SB ideal of preaching of his day from dramatic rhetorical style to an expository style of preaching.[15] He influenced the most prominent and renowned nineteenth century SB Greek and New Testament scholar A.T. Robertson who claimed:

> The world has never seemed the same to me since Broadus passed on. For ten years, I was enthralled by the witchery of his matchless personality. For three years, I was his assistant and colleague and for the part of the last year an inmate of his home. It was my sacred and sad privilege to see the passing of this

---

13. Dargan, "Baptist Pulpit," 404.
14. Moody, *Oral History Interview*, 13.
15. Mueller, *History of Southern Baptist*, 67.

prince in Israel. No man has ever stirred my nature as Broadus did in the classroom and in the pulpit. It has been my fortune to hear Beecher and Phillips Brooks, McLaren, Joseph Parker and Spurgeon, John Hall and Moody, John Clifford, and David Lloyd George. At his best and in a congenial atmosphere Broadus was the equal of any man that I have ever heard.[16]

Broadus's influence was significant because he was able to connect with both Northerners and Southerners and preached to people of all social classes. The invitation Broadus received to deliver the Lyman Beecher lectures on preaching at Yale Divinity School in 1889 was a signal of his national status. When the Sunday School Board (now LifeWay Christian Resources) was organized in 1891 the first publication project was *A Catechism of Bible Teaching* by John Broadus.

Broadus articulated his commitment and the importance of preaching in the introductory portion of his treatise on expository preaching. Broadus believed that preaching is the only causative mode for effecting salvation and transformation in life of congregants and the local church. Broadus was convinced that doctrine should be taught and sanctification can only be truly experienced when confronted with the texts of Scripture through proper expository preaching. Broadus asserted that preaching then is the sole, distinctive means for communicating or transmitting divine truth and that pastors and theologians should be adequately prepared to lead and influence their congregation.[17]

Broadus outlines his methodology for expository preaching and refers to the importance of being text-centered, engaging in the exegetical study of the biblical languages, and presenting the original meaning of the text to the congregants with the expectation of the likelihood for a transformative personal or societal life change.[18] Broadus's approach makes it normative for SB preachers to use the text as their main message or as the basis of their central sermonic ideas as they preach text-based sermons. SB seminary students, graduates, pastors, and theologians are trained with this model in mind to ensure they become expositors.

All SB seminaries and entities adhere to the principles of expository preaching. All SB seminaries require students to be taught the methodology of expository sermons. Denominational leaders are expected to be expository preachers and to uphold biblical inerrancy, infallibility, and inspiration. They are rigidly dogmatic about the idea of the authority and transformative

16. Robertson, *Minister*.
17. Broadus, *Treatise*, 2–3.
18. Broadus, *Treatise*, 2–3.

power of the scriptural text. The intrinsic authority and infallibility to which they ascribe the text has the resultant effect of causing them to want to see its standards adapted in popular culture or to influence society in general.

Broadus and Southern Seminary, the first seminary founded by the SBC, strongly influenced expository preaching, leading to the method's indoctrination into succeeding seminaries. Broadus's homiletic strategy also became instrumental in the move away from purely rhetorical presentations focused on pathos, logos, and ethos in the pulpit and toward creating emotive or sensationalistic responses in the polity. Broadus contended against the sheer use oratorical skills.[19] Furthermore, Broadus maintained that the sermon should move from explanation of the text to practical application in that the sermon should lead the congregant to act or live based on the original intent or meaning of the text. The sermon should call for a response. For Broadus, sermons must include practical acts or behavioral changes that line-up with scriptural text from its original form.

Broadus's methodology leads to expository sermons being the source for mobilizing the congregation and the centerpiece of a convert's spiritual experience. The sermon and the worship experience represent the all-important moments in the life of an SBC congregant. These are the moments in which congregants hear from God about His will and purposes for their lives. The expository sermon is the expression of the original intent and meaning of the text as God intended it and the text is inherently true. The expository preacher functions as a prophet who generates a salient expectancy in the congregant to respond positively to biblical text. However, the extent to which the expositor is deemed successful depends on his ability to effectively explain biblical meaning and engagingly or compellingly show its contemporary application.[20]

Broadus's mark on SB preaching and theology was brought to the fore when Professor Crawford Howell Toy studied at the University of Berlin from 1866 to 1868 and was a professor at the Southern Baptist Theological Seminary in Louisville, Kentucky. Toy served on the faculty of Southern Seminary in 1869 as a Professor of Old Testament Interpretation and Oriental Languages. Toy was influenced by the concept of higher criticisms, and in particular, by the influence of European theologians; later, Toy was dismissed from the seminary because of his intellectual ideologies. Toy was heavily influenced by Julius Wellhausen's historical-critical method of examining the Scriptures. Toy embraced the idea that New Testament writers incorrectly used a rabbinical hermeneutic methodology when including or

---

19. Broadus, *Treatise*, 2–3.
20. Broadus, *Treatise*, 333–35.

referencing Old Testament Scriptures in the New Testament. Toy asserted that the Bible has both a human and a divine element, but he also argued that the Bible has element of human fallibility that includes both error and myth. Broadus fervidly disagreed with Toy's hermeneutic view of inspiration.

Broadus responded to Toy with a treatise supporting the infallibility and inerrancy of the orthodox conservative view of biblical inspiration. Broadus authored the *Paramount and Permanent Authority of the Bible* and affirmed both the Bible's divine authorship and the infallibility of human authorship. In the *Paramount and Permanent Authority of the Bible*, Broadus asserted that the Bible does not contain the word of God because the Bible *is* the Word of God and truthful in all aspects. Broadus's view of the Scripture ultimately influenced the SBC, its seminaries, and a generation of pastors and theologians. The seminary maintained a conservative stance regarding inspiration, inerrancy, and infallibility and dissociated themselves and purged from the faculty all variant theological views. During the denominational struggle of the 1960s and 1970s, W. A. Criswell, Paige Patterson, and other conservative leaders referred to Broadus's theological views and practice to formulate a position based on his long-held premises. The conservative resurgence in the SBC reflected a similar exclusion of faculty, leadership which held diverse theological views, especially ones that disagreed with conservative understanding of inerrancy, inspiration and infallibility.

The Connection Between Faith and Preaching

Conservative orthodox theologians and preachers have asserted that the preaching or proclaiming the Word of God is a necessary for igniting faith (belief or confidence in God), which makes possible obedience and personal and community transformative behaviors. They point to the letter to the Heb 11:6 (NIV) that "without faith it is impossible to please God, because anyone who comes to him must believe that he exists and that he rewards those who earnestly seek him." Ryken, Wilhoit, Longman, Duriez, Penney, and Reid concluded the following:

> Hebrews 11 offers a complete catalogue of the heroes and heroines of faith, but even he runs out of time to list them all (Heb 11:32). The lives of these men and women show that faith is an unshakable belief that God will do everything he has promised to do even before there is visible evidence to that effect.[21]

---

21. Ryken et al., *Dictionary of Biblical Imagery*, 262.

According to SBC theologians and pastors, faith is absolutely necessary in order to know and have a personal relationship with God, and it can only be kindled through an interaction with the scriptural texts. There is a belief that the Scriptures affirms that only through the proclamation of the Word and positive response to it is there any sense of personal metamorphosis. Biblical preaching then should be the catalyst of personal and societal transformation.[22] Cranfield commented on the text of Romans speaking of believing a message as follows:

> A message's being believed involves an intermediate occurrence between the message's being uttered and its being believed, namely, its being heard. So in [verse] 17, Paul draws out (ἄρα) what is implied in his quotation, applying it to the matter in hand. Faith results from hearing the message, and the hearing of the message comes about through the word of Christ (i.e., through Christ's speaking the message by the mouths of His messengers).[23]

Robert Mounce too affirmed the role of preaching as tantamount to causing faith and ultimately obedience to God:

> Although it is true that faith is our response to the gospel, it is also true that the message itself awakens and makes faith possible. God is at work even in our response to his gracious offer of forgiveness. The message is heard "through the word of Christ," that is, it is Christ himself who speaks when the gospel is proclaimed. All effective preaching is accomplished by God himself. The messenger is at best merely the instrument used by the Holy Spirit as a necessary part of the process. It is God's own voice that confronts the sinner and offers reconciliation. This existential reality is what constitutes the gospel, "the power of God for . . . salvation" (Rom 1:16).[24]

Preaching then is absolutely necessary for traditional faith communities such as the SBC in which a syncretic relationship exists between faith and preaching. Additionally, the SBC understands that the outcome of preaching is first the result of the workings of faith through hearing the divine message.

---

22. Schreiner, *Romans*. 567–68.
23. Cranfield, *Critical and Exegetical Commentary*, 537.
24. Mounce, *Romans*, 212.

Establishing Hermeneutical Modes from the Old Testament

A critical component to the SBC belief in expository preaching is that they consider that it was the model practiced in the Old Testament. SBC expositors practice a methodology whereby the contemporary communication and contextualization of a scriptural text has its foundation in the exegetical process of moving from the original language to the re-expression or transference to the receptor culture. Unsurprisingly, they follow a hermeneutical model that is based on a biblical exegetical methodology model on particular scriptural texts which exemplify the act of interpretation and exposition. SBC preachers held the idea the experience of Ezra served as foundation story of expository preaching, particularly due to the need for translation and interpretation in the task of expository preaching.

The books of Ezra and Nehemiah recount the post-exilic return from the Babylonian captivity. The captivity of the Southern Kingdom by the Neo-Babylonian Empire is dated from 605–539 BC. The period of captivity lasted for seventy years and their resurgence and initial departure from the subsequent Medes-Persian Empire occurred in a series of three primary excursions back to their homeland. There were three distinct departures the first is recorded in Ezra 1:1 led by Sheshbazzar, the second occurred in the seventh year of Artaxerxes Longimanus, approximately eight years later (Ezra 7:7), under the leadership of Ezra. The third wave of return stemmed thirteen years after the second, in the twentieth year of Artaxerxes Longimanus, directed and led my Nehemiah (Neh 2:1). The size and population of Judah was indiscriminately smaller in the post-exilic period and the time in captivity for the first time in their history ushered in a shift in their ability to understand the original Hebrew text of the Old Testament. They had adopted the Aramaic language of the Babylonian empire.

The post-exilic immigrants had adopted the Aramaic language of their subjugators and were in need of a translator or a translation that would convey the unadulterated meaning of the Hebrew text. In this regard the SB expositor faces a similar dilemma as he has to interpret an ancient text that was written Hebrew or Greek which he has to translate in order to convey the original meaning of the text. The SB conviction regarding antiquity, orthodoxy, catholicity, inspiration and inerrancy demands that he uncovers or interpret the original meaning of the text. Expository preaching has the expectancy of accuracy and untainted. The SBC congregants like the post-exilic assume that they are hearing the original text and its application for contemporary time.

The ascendancy of the role of the post-exilic translator or communicator inadvertently arose out of each particular historical situation. Furthermore, there was a connection between obedience to the scriptural text and welfare of the returnees. Historically, adherence to the scriptural text led to a belief that the Jewish nation would experience prosperity, personal success, divine presence, and not just an ephemeral experience of God's omnipresence. The exposition of the biblical texts during the post-exilic period was viewed as the only means of ensuring the accurate rendering of the texts and the practical implementation of its tenets. Furthermore, due to the disobedience of the Old Testament Laws divine retribution occurred and led to the seventy-year captivity.

The text indicates that after the walls of Jerusalem were rebuilt following to its destruction during the siege of 605 BC the remnant men and women met together probably at the Water Gate of the outskirts of the temple since only men were allowed in the temple. The text identifies book to be read as the "the Book of the Law." Despite the Babylonian captivity, there is importance attached to the book associated with Moses, the chief lawgiver in Jewish history, as either all or part of the Pentateuch is read to the people. The congregation was comprised of men, women, and children, and the latter group is indicated through the use of the expression "any capable of understanding what they heard." The root word used for "understand" is ןיב and is repeated in verses seven to nine to underscore the idea of giving or conveying the meaning of something and to make it clear. Segments or parts of the biblical texts were "read from" (קרא ב), and a large platform was erected for the proclamation of the text (לדבר = "for the purpose") as the immense size of the congregation warranted a visible presence to ensure the congregants could receive the auditory communication of the texts.

Ezra, the priests, and leaders in the community were accompanied on the platform by thirteen additional leaders who represented the laity. The text asserts that Ezra "Opened the book" (חתפיו רפסה), which means, he literally unrolled the scroll. Ezra began his exposition with benedictory expressions of praise "to the great God" (הלאהי הגדול), and the congregation responded with a shout of "Amen!" as they lifted their hands in worship and reverence. Verses seven and ight both reveal that the Levites assisted Ezra with the exposition of the original text. As Ezra read the text in the hearing of the people, the Levites provided detailed explanation.

The text reads that the Levites were "giving the sense" (an infinitive absolute), and the resultant effect was that the members of the community were able to understand the textual reading. The role of the Levites operated in tandem with other scriptural references which detailed their responsibilities (Deut 33:10; 2 Chr 17:7–9; 35:3). The text was read by Ezra and, the

Levites and the congregants "understood the reading," which caused them to weep. Ezra apparently selected the text and provided a clear explanation and application, thus making the text relevant to his hearers.

Ezra used the expositional, hermeneutical and expository model to make applicable the demands of historically obsolete laws. The conclusion of the reading and exposition came with an exhortatory statement: "It is the joy of the Lord that is your protection." Ezra attempted to convey to the congregation that they need not fear the wrath or judgment that may ensue from God because of disobedience. Ezra declared that "The joy of the Lord" was the through the celebration and worship of God and that each Israelite would experience God's protection if they listened to and obeyed the Scriptures.

Ezra employed a hermeneutic which focused on selecting certain texts, reading them in the original, but then explaining the texts in such a way that the people could understand their divine messages. In the Old Testament, the prophets mostly focused on aspects the law that included the Ten Commandments and the standards for various seasonal feasts, worship, cultic rituals, and celebrations. Ezra explained historical text but showed its relevance to the modern hearers.

The Israelites were stunned when they saw their clear lack of obedience in light of the divine demands. Their fear of retribution led them to recommit to their worship and celebration of God. They demonstrated a commitment to the biblical texts, and it was equally noticeable that the congregants were comprised men, women, and children, thereby ensuring no generational disparity in the dissemination of the biblical texts. This text thus serves a pivotal model for the formation of a methodology dedicated to exegesis of original texts and for contemporizing biblical meaning to be relevant to hearers.

The apparent effect of Ezra's expository method was a community response which engendered both fear and worship of God. The theological assumption is that a repentant community offers witness, experiences divine protection, and receives providential help. Therefore, Ezra's hermeneutic produced a community committed to obeying the biblical standard and engaging in worship, celebration, and the expectancy that God would act on their behalf.

Benemann, the SB theologian and expositor examines this same text in the SBC's commentary series, *New American Commentary*. In his examination he asserts the importance of an exegetical study of the text. He also shows his commitment to determining the original meaning and the situation of the original audience. Breneman's examination not only demonstrates the exegetical methodology associated with expository preaching but also reveals his commitment to orthodox, conservative theology and his belief in the inerrancy of the text. His approach shows the interconnectedness between theology and the task of expository preaching. His expository methodology demands the examination of the original and then connect it with the situation of the contemporary audience.

Benemann's examination of the Nehemiah text is both performative and instructive. He attempts to utilize the expository methodology to determine meaning and reveals that the text is a validation of the SBC methodology of expository preaching. Benemann discusses the original situation of the Jewish exilic returnees and details their historical situation as the *Sizt im Leben*. At the same time that Benemann affirms SBC theological doctrines of orthodoxy and inspiration, he alludes to the necessity of the practical impartation of the text by its hearers of the community of faith. Benemann argues that this text shows the effect of expository preaching on mobilizing congregants to engage in cultic worship and how it can lead to a strong impassioned response by congregants. Benemann argues to for the authoritativeness of the scriptural text and asserts that the task of exegesis and exposition is somewhat arduous. Benemann claims that the task of expository preaching involves translation, interpretation, and linguistic analysis. Benemann illustrates the exegetical effort in which SBC's theologians and pastors engage and reveals the emphasis that is placed on the authority and inspiration of the Scriptures because of the perceived role God plays in the living faith community as outlined in his exegesis of the text.[25]

The prominent expositor, homiletician, mentor, and model for many SB and conservative preachers, Stephen F. Alford, cites this passage as the primary Old Testament theological textual evidence for expository preaching.[26] Both Benemann and Alford affirm the SBC belief in authority, inspiration, and inerrancy. They each argue for the necessity of expository preaching in the context of determining and explaining the meaning of the text to the contemporary congregations because the text is written in a foreign language. There is a need to expound theological doctrines and make practical applications from the text in anticipation of transformative or sanctification in the life of congregants. There is also a linguistic gap that makes expository preaching all the more necessary. The text of the Old Testament was originally written in ancient Hebrew and Aramaic and the New Testament was written in Koine Greek. These are languages that are not commonly known or widely taught. Few people have an understanding of Hebrew and Greek, let alone the linguistic attributes of these languages.

25. Breneman, *Ezra, Nehemiah, Esther*, 223–28.
26. Olford and Olford, *Anointed Expository Preaching*, 69–71.

Ironically, SBC congregants look to these same texts for personal, spiritual guidance for their whole lives. The text which is believed to be inspired and authoritative is written in ancient language which contemporary congregants cannot understand. This lack of understanding of ancient languages necessitates the work of translation as a part of the process of the expository exegetical methodology. Broadus's focus on the original languages highlights expository necessity and the work of Broadus's disciple A. T. Robertson.

Robertson was very concerned that the exposition of the biblical text includes a careful exegesis or study of the grammar, historicity and lexical meaning of the original languages. In Robertson's preface to the *Grammar of the Greek New Testament in the Light of Historical Research*, he wrote the following:

> This Grammar aims to keep in touch at salient points with the results of comparative philology and historical grammar as the true linguistic science. In theory one should be allowed to assume all this in a grammar of the Greek N. T., but in fact that cannot be done unless the book is confined in use to a few technical scholars.[27]

Robertson asserted that it was important to study the original language of the New Testament, which is Koine Greek, in conjunction with a historical study of the Greek culture. Thus, historical, grammatical, and lexical study became an important aspect of biblical exegesis. Robertson engages in the study of word formations and examines etymology, root-forms, parts of speech, orthography, phonetics, declensions, and the conjugation of verb forms.[28]

Robertson's grammatical analysis is foundational to his methodology of uncovering the precise meanings of the words and meanings in the text because he examined the syntax of the text. Robertson found the following from his examination of syntax:

> The distinctive character of the N. T. teaching is more closely allied to lexicography and syntax than to mere forms. That is very true, but many a theologian's syntax has run away with him and far from the sense of the writer, because he was weak on the mere forms. Knowledge of the forms is the first great step toward syntax."[29]

---

27. Robertson, "Analytical Grammar."
28. Robertson, "Analytical Grammar."
29. Robertson, "Analytical Grammar."

Robertson argued that the use of syntax was for both "construction of the single word and for clauses." Robertson added:

> One must admit the difficulty of the whole question and not conceive that the ancients ran a sharp line between the form and the meaning of the form. But, all in all, it is more scientific to gather the facts of usage first and then interpret these facts. This interpretation is scientific syntax, while the facts of usage are themselves syntax. Thus considered one may properly think of syntax in relation to the words themselves, the forms of the words, the clauses and sentences, the general style.[30]

Moreover, Robertson's exegetical methodology included an examination of the tense, voice and mood of Greek words, particles and figures of speech.[31] Robertson used this methodological approach to establish a thorough analysis of the original language of the New Testament and the expression of its meaning through the process of expositional preaching. Robertson's text and approach became standard use at SBC seminaries and became a vital component of the process of expository preaching. Robertson's commitment to his exegetical process as a means of communicating the intended meaning of the original is seen in his publication of the verse by verse, presentation of word pictures of the original Greek of the New Testament to bring to light the words and actions of early Christians.

Robertson believed in the practice of textual criticism. His detailed approached to biblical exegesis was warranted because of his concern with exposing the meaning of the text albeit even in situations when there were variant readings of copies of the original manuscripts. Robertson wrote *An Introduction to the Textual Criticism of the New Testament* whereby he sought to both personally determine and to influence his SBC seminary students to study the original language of the New Testament using the methodology of literary criticism. His purpose was to make certain that they have the "purest text possible" as they exegete and exposit the original language of the text.[32]

Robertson described the type of peaching that is reflective of a thoroughgoing exegetical and literary analysis. He recognizes the first century preacher Apollos as one the great expositors of all time and connects Apollos's preaching with a strong emphasis on the exegetical and homiletic methodology, "the last lecture that Broadus delivered to his New Testament class in the Southern Baptist Theological Seminary was on Apollos. He made a

---

30. Robertson, "Analytical Grammar."
31. Robertson, "Analytical Grammar."
32. Robertson, *Introduction to the Textual Criticism*, 37.

thrilling appeal to young ministers to be "mighty in the Scriptures. It is not possible to be powerful in the use of the Scriptures without an adequate knowledge of the books of Scripture. One, if possible, should have technical acquaintance with the problems of scholar ship, the language, the history, the religious ideas, the social conditions, the relations to other religions and peoples, the development in response to new ideas, the transforming power of Christ's life and teachings upon mankind."[33] Robertson also associates good preaching with the ability to encourage and console the audience as he also identifies the New Testament apostle Barnabas as a model preacher, "Luke translates Barnabas by "son of exhortation" though the Greek covers also the ideas of consolation and of encouragement. There is no English word that can carry all these ideas, and we face the same difficulty with the term "Paraclete" for the Holy Spirit." Robertson sees value in recognizing the qualities, characters and style of Apollos as exemplifying good preaching.

Robertson saw the value of interpretation and translation, in his preface to the Grammar of the Greek New Testament when he stated, "Perhaps those who pity the grammarian do not know that he finds joy in his task and is sustained by the conviction that his work is necessary."[34] SB assert that Robertson wrote the seminal text on the lexical-grammatical study of New Testament Greek based on a belief that the expositor must bridge the gap between the original language and the receptor culture. SBC theologians and pastors argue for the centrality of the text and so the task of translating the text is an important aspect of the exegetical process and the expository methodology. The SBC expository is seemingly obligated to translate or use a translation that reflects a literal reading of the text. The text that is used to frame the sermon and the translation used should be accurate in its rendering of the original for the SBC this means that the expositor should examine the language of the original in order to understand and preach based on the literal meaning of the text. It is their goal that their congregants hear the original rendering and understanding its original meaning as the transformative authority comes from the original meaning of the text.

The complexity that SB face is that the Old Testament was written in Hebrew and Aramaic and that the original manuscripts have been lost and so we only have copies of the original autographs which are too translations of the original. Furthermore, the Jesus of the New Testament and his apostles spoke Aramaic and Greek and so Jesus's words and the apostles included translations of the original. The expositor then has the task of interpreting and translating texts that are really translations of the original.

33. Roberston, *Types of Preachers*, 16.
34. Robertson, *Grammar of the Greek*, ix.

The expositor because of his exegetical methodology asserts that there is a need to remain as close to the original as possible. This is the central goal expository preaching and that's the foremost purpose of SB expositors. Also, SBC congregations have to expect and believe that their pastors and theologians would practice the expository methodology.

Robertson contends that the language of the New Testament is multifaceted, Jesus and the apostles in some cases trilingual and so the writers of the scriptural texts and subsequent copyist had to translate the original speech or words. Additionally, the use of the OT represents a translation and interpretation on their part. The SB expositor has to investigate the Greek rendering, and in some cases, the Greek rendering of the original translation. Robertson and SBC expository preachers have examined etymology, semantics, syntax, and genre in order to understand the original meaning of words and phrases as the root occurrence of words and phrases to interpret and present the original meaning of the text. Robertson's approach has become normative in the hermeneutic model of expository preaching. His grammar outlined in detail the literary analytical approach that expositors should embody.

However, Robertson's and the SBC approach sill utilized a theological grid in their hermeneutic model. Their methodology emphasized the need to maintain a commitment to the doctrinal belief in the authority and inspiration of the scriptural text. In essence, Robertson's exegetical methodology assumed that the original meaning supported orthodox doctrine. Therefore, the doctrines about Scripture arising out of the study of systematic and biblical theology served as means of ensuring that the translation and interpretation was consistent with orthodoxy. The task of translation and interpretation for SBC expositors was obligated to maintain a fidelity to orthodox doctrine. This in some ways limited the task of translation or restricted the translation or interpretation choices of a scriptural regardless of the evidence of the exegetical analysis. Nonetheless, Robertson's *Grammar of the Greek New Testament in the Light of Historical Research* which was published in 1914 was extolled by world scholars Adolf Deissmann, F. W. Grossheide, and Edgar J. Goodspeed. Robertson's methodology and influence would be seen in his classroom especially in one of his students, Dr. W. A. Criswell, who wrote that Robertson "was the greatest scholar under whom it was ever my privilege to study. His way of teaching did not inspire me so much as it frightened me into hours and hours of studying."[35]

Dr. W. A. Criswell would in turn influence a generation of SBC expositors and pastors and would play a leading role in the conservative

---

35. Jones, "New Testament," 23.

resurgence in the SBC. Criswell would also establish the Criswell College, an undergraduate and graduate SBC entity with a commitment to teaching expository preaching, affirming social conservative values and upholding the SBC doctrines of Scripture. Criswell is considered one of the foremost SBC expositors, mega-church pastors and denominational leader. In a lecture delivered at the Criswell College. W. A. Criswell too accentuated the need for expository preaching and its positive effect based on the text of Nehemiah 8 and highlighted its significance for emphasizing the necessity and effectiveness of expository preaching.

Criswell too emphasized the need to engage in expository preaching however, he exposed a more pastoral or homiletic concern. Criswell asserted for the need for clarity and connected this concept with the experience of the exiles who were presented with an account of the original with explanations to clarify the meaning of the text. Criswell saw the task of the expositor as a necessary role to convey the meaning of the original to receptor audience because of the linguistic gap that existed. Criswell asserted to that the exposition should lead to a response from the congregation, there should be a level of mobilization, the movement of the congregation to the act on the sermon. This is a mark of SBC expository preaching in that the sermon should solicit a response from the congregation either personally or corporately. Criswell believed that the congregation inherently desire to the exposition of the text he had theological reasons for this belief, but his intent is to shape the congregation so that the adopted the doctrinal and theological elements of the texts and act accordingly. Ultimately, Criswell saw the expository sermon as an instrument for transmitting theological doctrines but also for engendering a positive response and commitment to the tenets of the expository sermon and in so doing mobilize the local congregation.

Establishing Hermeneutical Modes from the New Testament

SB theologians have referred 2 Tim 2:15 as a model text for asserting that the New Testament hermeneutic supports an sermonic methodology. 2 Tim 2:15 which in the manuscript of the Greek text reads, "Be diligent to present yourself approved to God as a workman who does not need to be ashamed, accurately handling the word of truth." The text reveals that there is a theological connection between the qualitative character of the decoder of the biblical text and accurately communicating the text. Through the use of an imperative σπούδασον, which has the sense of "being persistently eager and zealous" to denote the initiative that should characterize the teacher of a biblical text. In so doing, through the use of an infinitive clause, (σεαυτὸν δόκιμον παραστῆσαι τῷ θεῷ), the exegete and communicator will literally "show or present yourself approved to God." The word for present "παραστῆσαι" means "becomes almost equivalent to," the communicator of the Scriptures is mandated to interpret exegete and translate the text in such a manner so that he or she corroborates their divine calling and acceptance.

The manner in which the exegete is demanded to operate is rendered by the phrase, ἐργάτης ἀνεπαίσχυντον, literally, "a worker unapologetic or unashamed." Hence the interpreter of the text is considered as engaging in a laborious task to ensure that the dissemination of the text is of highest quality soἀνεπαίσχυντον (a NT hapax; means "unashamed"). The word ὀρθοτομέω means literally "cut straight" or "cut right." The emphasis is that the worker or exegete laboriously seeks to "get it right" and to accurately render the meaning of the original. The work or "cutting right" or expositing is deemed an arduous task, but the expositor deals carefully with "the word of truth" (τὸν λόγον τῆς ἀληθείας) that is the text of Scripture. The interpreter of Scripture should work diligently to ensure that the text is accurately studied so that its meaning and intention is communicated properly.[36] It is the purview of the interpreter then to ensure that through meticulous analysis there an accurate rendering of the original. The expositor negates the efficacy of the task of translating and communicating whenever there a schism between original text and translation. Paul asserts then that this function of the expositor is both a divine calling and responsibility. The dominant SBs theologians and expositors subscribe this hermeneutic philosophy which undergirds their demand for commitment to expository sermons.

Dr. Criswell emphasized the importance of engaging in careful exegesis and homiletics. Criswell asserts that it is the responsibility of the expositor to present the theological doctrines to the congregants. His comments here are homiletic and show the practical ideas of the text. Criswell here moved from exegesis to homiletics in order to emphasize the contemporary connection or relevance. However, Criswell engaged in not just historical exegesis but also canonical exegesis. He utilized historical exegesis in that he examined the various historical interpretations of the text by religious scholars dating from the first century but he also interpreted the text based on its context and location in biblical canon and how it was viewed by the original audience. His methodology reveals a deeper commitment to making connections with other biblical text in order to support his original exegetical points. He does follow the historical theological stances of Broadus and A. T. Robertson. He reveals a commitment to inspiration, orthodoxy

---

36. Knight, *Pastoral* Epistles, 411–12.

and canonicity. In essence, he adopts their perspective and uses it as a means of engaging in canonical theology, he references the text that connect philologically and theologically with his primary text.

Criswell's exposition does not necessarily reveal or showcase his literal-grammatical exegetical analysis, but the outcome of his exegesis is a homiletic that coveys the main idea of the text with other canonical support. Criswell utilized the expository methods in his pastoral and pulpit ministry while serving as the pastor of the historic First Baptist Church (FBC) Dallas for over fifty years and as pastor emeritus until his death. Criswell was credited with establishing the megachurch model for the SBC. Through his preaching ministry, publication he was responsible for starting a religious radio station that broadcasted pastors with a penchant for effective expositions, the college he founded, Criswell Bible College was not just dedicated to teaching biblical studies and how to exposit the sermon. Criswell College was also a beginning point for many leaders who would take on SBC denominational leadership positions, and leadership role in SBC entities and seminaries. Denominational leaders such David Allen, Paige Patterson, Danny Akin, Richard Melick Jr., Jerry Johnson, and Richard Wells all served at or attended Criswell College. Also, many denominational leaders served under Criswell's leadership on staff at FBC Dallas or at some point served as a pastor of the church such O. S. Hawkins, Mac Brunson and Robert Jeffress.

Criswell's influence is extensive. By using the practice of expository preaching, Criswell successfully mobilized his congregation to become one of the most influential, largest, and wealthiest in the United States.[37] Criswell's expository method was not just a rigid explanation of the text, but his approach integrated passion, humor, vivid illustrations, and extemporaneous communication.[38]

Dr. David Allen served as a senior pastor at the SBC church and as the Dean of the School of Theology, Professor of Preaching, Director of the Southwestern Center for Expository Preaching, and George W. Truett Chair of Ministry at Criswell College. Allen also develops a similar New Testament hermeneutic by emphasizing the importance of validating the original meaning of the text and striving to communicate the meaning and intent of the textual author. Allen accentuated the need to examine the depth of the original meaning and to convey it in a manner in which relevantly connects with a given audience. Essentially, the expositor should endeavor to gain the original intended meaning and purposefully engage recipients with practical principles.

37. Criswell, *Why I Preach*.
38. Toulouse, "W. A. Criswell"; McBeth, *First Baptist Church of Dallas*.

Allen is extremely meticulous in his exegetical approach by focusing on the historical context, engaging in a literary-grammatical analysis, and examining the syntax and specific semantic domains of the text. Allen follows the methodology of A. T. Robertson to study the original Greek text and understanding it according to the purpose of the original meaning. Allen works toward understanding the genre and more so than did Broadus, but Allen's process of discovery and analysis is somewhat similar to Criswell's by involving canonical exegesis. It is apparent that based on Allen's homiletic approach, he subscribes to inerrancy, canonicity, and inspiration so he values the responsibility, demands and obligation to exposit the text. Allen, like Broadus, believes that the text should drive the sermon, in that the original meaning of the text should extrapolated and presented to the contemporary audience. What is significant about Allen's approach is that he believes in the doing the work of translation and understand the necessity to translate or interpret as close to original as possible.

Allen teaches this methodology at Southwestern Baptist Theological Seminary and he did the same at Criswell College where he was the department chair of expository preaching. Allen also propagates this methodology in his publications and lectures at SBC meetings, conferences and seminars. Additionally, it is very striking that Allen believes that the main or controlled verbs should drive or serve as the central idea(s) of the sermon. Allen's approach is fully reliant on the text to shape the sermon but not just through the communication of the original meaning but that the structure of the original should be presented to the congregants or the audience. In other words, for Allen the original language shapes the structure of the sermon, the main points and practical application. Allen's approach is distinctive in his overt reliance and use of the original text. Allen pushes the limits in expressing the original, he does not want to lose the structure, flow or transitions in the text. All linguistic aspects should be expressed in the text. He does follow a homiletic that attempts to make the text relevant and applicable and believes that the text should be engaging for the contemporary audience. However, the exposits has to work within the framework of the original as the indicator of the sermon structure and the sermon points or ideas and in so doing allow the sermon to speak to the congregants utilizing the voice of the original.

The Southern Baptist Convention and Hermeneutic Modes

In 1859, James P. Boyce founded the Southern Baptist Theological Seminary in Greenville, SC. Southern was the first seminary in the South. Along with

Broadus and later A. T. Robertson and the early faculty of the Southern Seminary they developed a seminary model for training and educating pastors and preachers particularly in the area of expository preaching. Their belief in expository preaching and the commitment of the SBC to the doctrine of inspiration, inerrancy and infallibility has made expository preaching a necessity and standard part of the all SBC seminary curriculum. It is primarily through the seminaries and SBC colleges that they have influenced pastors and denominational leaders. Boyce believed that a Southern seminary would be able to prepare men who could preach the gospel in the familiar New Testament mantra of "a workman that need not to be ashamed." This quotation was frequently used to support the notion that the preacher or pastor should be highly educated and equipped to exegete and teach the Scriptures. Boyce was particularly interested in addressing the problem of inadequate preaching and poor pastoral and ministerial preparation which he considered prevalent evil in his address. Furthermore, Boyce contended that a properly trained minister who is skilled in the practice and preparation of expository sermons, that this minister would significantly improve the spiritual life of his congregation and the denomination as a whole. Boyce also stated, "And while our denomination has continued to increase, and our principles have annually been spreading more widely, it has been sensibly felt that whatever ministerial increase has accompanied has been not only disproportionate to that of our membership but has owed its origin in not respect to the influence of theological education." Boyce believed here that a solid theological education would include teaching ministers how to exposit the Bible and preach expository sermons. Accordingly, for a Boyce a Southern seminary would rejuvenate the ministries and outreach activities of the Southern churches specifically through the preaching of the Bible, which he saw as desperate need for the SBC denomination.[39]

The evangelization of the South was of great concern to SB theologians and pastors as well as Boyce. They saw the need to affect social change by preaching the Bible and realizing the transformation of the existing culture. This burden continues, and SB have consistently relied on expository preaching not just to train the congregants but to mobilize their congregants to bring about social change. Boyce's concept of a seminary education was also founded on the principle that ministers should be trained in a manner which is more relevant to their situation and not necessarily follows the tenets of the classical education of the universities of his day. Boyce asserted that SBC seminaries should specifically teach and show seminary students in real, practical and helpful ways as to how to care for congregants, preach

---

39. Wills, *Southern Baptist Theological Seminary*, 13–22.

and manage the church.⁴⁰ Boyce sought to maintain a markedly doctrinally sound denomination which was committed to preparing ministers (who may have been unable to afford a purely secular, classical education). Along with fellow Baptist leaders Boyce were keen on ensuring that SB pastors were trained to exegete the Scriptures, preach the texts, and teach in churches. They believed that the ministers if provided with a clear understanding of Baptist history and polity were effectively led and impart Baptists beliefs to their congregants. Boyce wanted to, ensure the longevity and transformation of existing culture thereby making possible a clear demarcation with other denominations and solidify Baptist theology in the SB pews.

J. P. Boyce along with other SB pastors, namely Basil Manly, Jr., formulated a doctrinal statement to represent the shared theological values and biblical commitment of the founding faculty. Together they wrote the Abstract of Principles that formed the theological doctrinal statement of faith for many of SBC seminaries and colleges. Basil Manly, Jr., was a fellow Princeton professor. Manly worked solely on the first draft of document during the spring of 1858 that contained twenty articles. Manly presented his work to the SBC committee responsible for the final formation of the statement. The SBC committee gathered in May 1858 at the SBC's plan of organization meeting in Greenville. Manly, Boyce, along with John Broadus, E. T. Winkler, and William Williams completed the final draft of the document. These SB leaders used the 1689 London Baptist Confession of Faith, the Westminster Confession, the Philadelphia Confession, and the 1833 New Hampshire Confession as the framework for developing and defining the final twenty articles.⁴¹ The abstract was ratified by the SBC in 1858, a year before Southern Seminary opened, to be officially accepted as part of the seminary's official creed. The hallmark of the abstract was the seminary's assurance that it would make certain that its professors were faithful in proclaiming SB beliefs and principles with aligned with the Scriptures and to reiterate the idea that the seminary existed to serve the local church and not to replace it. The charter is distinctively Calvinistic not only because of the theological leanings of its authors but also due to the utilization of various historical documents such as the 1689 London Baptist Confession of Faith, the Westminster Confession, the Philadelphia Confession, and the 1833 New Hampshire Confession. The latter creeds were founded on pure Calvinistic principles and became a hallmark of not only the theological position of SB theologians and pastors but also were reflected in the hermeneutical practices of the SBC.

40. Wills, *Southern Baptist Theological Seminary*.
41. Wills, *Southern Baptist Theological Seminary*.

Pivotal to the development on the SBC's Calvinistic theological and hermeneutical principles was John Leadley Dagg. Dagg was a member of the Executive Committee of the Georgia Baptist Convention, and he subsequently elected to the Constitution Committee of the SBC at its first meeting in Augusta, Georgia in 1844. He also served as president of Haddington College, Alabama Female Athenaeum, and Mercer University. Dagg wrote his "Manual of Theology" which was first published in 1857, which later became the main systematic theological textbook for the first twenty-five years of Southern Seminary. It predated J.P. Boyce's *Abstract of Systematic Theology* which later became the standard theological textbook used by the seminary. Dagg also wrote on church organizational structure and ecclesiology in *A Treatise on Church Order* (1858), morality in *The Elements of Moral Science* (1859), and on and apologetics in *The Evidences of Christianity* (1869). All of which were used as textbooks in the early used of the seminary as well us throughout SBC seminaries.

Dagg was a staunch inerrantist, having been strongly influenced through Calvin's belief in verbal plenary inspiration and his concept of divine revelation. Dagg believed that the Bible was the primary means of knowing and experiencing God. Further, he asserted that the Bible was transmitted from God to human beings. Dagg clarified this view by stating that inspiration implies that the Scriptures faithfully convey or accurately render the occasion, setting, verbal communication through the human personalities or authors of Scripture. For Dagg, reading the Scriptures is in fact an encounter with God and so it is vitally necessary to precisely read, interpret and understand the Scriptures as they are the very words of God to human beings.[42] Dagg's view of Scriptures superimposed a certain hermeneutic methodology. Dagg averred that the Scriptures should be read in the public hearing and that the text of Scriptures should be interpreted, explained and given practical applications to the life of the congregants. Dagg referenced the standard text for expositing the Scriptures.[43] Additionally, Dagg believed that the ability to interpret and teach the word was contingent on a special divine calling and hence involves a supernatural endowment.[44] Dagg asserted that a true follower of the Christian faith, a Baptist, will ensure that he or she fully follows and obeys the Scriptures. The SBC preacher must be determined and devoted to proclaiming the Word of God to bring about life change amongst the congregations.

---

42. Wills, *Southern Baptist Theological Seminary*, 13–22.
43. Wills, *Southern Baptist Theological Seminary*, 13–22.
44. Wills, *Southern Baptist Theological Seminary*, 13–22.

Dagg believed the Baptist preacher had special calling to ensure obedience to the biblical text. In addition, the SBC preacher had an integral role in making sure that fellow Baptists and the denomination at large did not waver from traditional SBC beliefs or compromise its theological distinctiveness by adapting to social or cultural norms. Dagg avowed that the SBC adherent and denomination should be undeterred by social or even legal practices which are in contradiction to its belief system. It the prerogative then for the Baptist preacher to safeguard doctrinal purity in the pews, through preaching in the pulpit and preparation in the seminary.

Whilst Dagg did not outline a procedural system for determining his theological outcomes, his system for interpretation is evident through systematic overview of biblical theology. Through his theological approach Dagg revealed his concern with ascertaining the lexical and grammatical meaning as well as the historical background of the text as he determines his theological position. In his discussion about baptism, Dagg referenced the cultural and historical understand of the terms for baptism and the lexical meanings of the word for baptism as proof for baptism by immersion. Dagg forwent the figurative or allegorical interpretation and instead relies on concrete literal interpretation to garner the meaning of the text.[45]

Broadly speaking SB theologians are leery of interpretative schemas that do not follow the literal or concrete interpretive model, such as moralistic interpretations of the text. Moralistic hermeneutics focuses on the interpreting the text with the intent on using the Bible to teach about faith as well as to provide guidance about daily conduct and decision making. For example Rabbi Hillel (late 1st century bc to early 1st century ad) established rules to ensure the collection of debts and the security of the economy even when allowing for the cancellation of debts based on the Old Testament.[46] SB theologians and pastors reject an anagogical (mystical or spiritual) interpretation of the text in which literal or concrete details receive a meaning spiritually and can be used to relate to future events or personal experiences. Once such example involves identifying with the Red Sea in the Old Testament as symbolic of difficulties, challenges, or experiences of pain, and another example involves referencing the parting of the Red Sea as symbolic of God's transition of believers from this earthly abode to an eternity in Heaven.[47]

Dagg was clearly committed to the exegetical analysis of the text before developing his theological positions. He focuses on the historical, lexical, and grammatical aspects of the text and rejects untoward figurative

---

45. Dagg, *Manual for Church Order*.
46. Talmud Bavli, Gittin 36a
47. Aquinas, *Summa Theologica*, Tertia Pars, 39.4.1.

interpretations of the texts. The men of the founding faculty of Southern seminary and their disciples follow the followed the methodology of exegesis and expository preaching. Their main concern is to garner the exact or precise original meaning of the text. They believe that the text has an implicit authority and veracity. If it is communicated, it will bring about life change and obeisance to the biblical ideas relevant to SBC doctrine and dogma.

Accordingly, SBC expositors are reluctant to follow the early patristic Alexandrian method of interpretation made popular by Philo (20 BC to AD 50) that was focused on the allegorical or metaphorical interpretation of the text. In the Alexandrian method, there were allegorical interpretations that draw parallels between biblical characters and Jesus or provide views of specific images or Old Testament ideas as pointing to Jesus Christ.[48] This method sought to spiritualize the text instead of examining the concrete or literal meaning of the text. SBC expositors avoid this methodology and do not want to incorporate it or aspects of its elements in its interpretative methodology.

SBC expositors, instead, utilize another patristic school of interpretation, the Antiochene, and concentrate on uncovering the literal meaning of the text.[49] The Antiochene methodology serves as the historical foundational basis for the expository methodology as seen in commentaries and work of its early practitioners such as John Chrysostom.[50] Later, the foremost Protestant preacher Martin Luther emphasized this methodology. His views on the interpretation of Scripture especially the Eucharist revealed a commitment to the literal interpretation of Scripture.[51]

The SBC aligned with the Antiochene methodology as it supported the expository methodology as providing an accurate rendering of the original and associating translations with the literal and concrete renderings of the original text.[52] The Alexandrian school formulated a methodology, which at times, included an exegetical analysis. However, the Alexandrian application and meaning was allegorical and lacked true authority based on SBC principles. The core of the appeal for expository preaching is the belief in a divine authority within the Old and New Testament texts and the implicit connection with patristic hermeneutics in a model focused on literal interpretation.[53] SBC theologians rely on a methodology that preserves the

48. Patapios, "Alexandrian," 187; Guillet quoted in Fairburn, "Patristic Exegesis," 8.
49. Thistleton, *Hermeneutics*, 106; Young, "Patristic Biblical Interpretation," 567.
50. Chrysostom, *Homily 15*.
51. Erickson, *Christian Theology*, 117.
52 Goldsworthy, "Biblical Theology and Hermeneutics," 3–16.
53. Goldsworthy, "Lecture 2: Biblical Theology," 31–32.

original intent of the text. Consequently, there is a strong devotion to the exegetical and expository methodology developed and refined by Broadus and other and now taught and practiced in most SBC seminaries.

Conclusion to the Historical Elements of Expository Preaching

The starting point for the SBC expository preaching methodology lies in their belief in the transformative and authoritative power of the scriptural text. Their arguments are somewhat circular in support of these theological tenets of the scriptural texts. The SBC pastors and theologians engage in the act of expository preaching as they believe that if congregants hear the originally inspired meaning of the text and the original voice of God, they will obey and adhere to God's teachings. SBC preachers contend that Scripture contains the very words of God and produce regeneration and sanctification. SBC theologians and pastors believe that the scriptural text itself is a witness to the cause and result of the supernatural experience of divine transformative power. It is imperative for SB expositors to present the actual and originally intended words of God. Anything less than a literal rendering of the original text within contemporary application dilutes or adulterates the scriptural text, which in itself is a violation of the scriptural text.

The SBC expositor takes great pains to discover the original and to present it to the congregants so that they can understand and obey the scriptural text. The congregants for generations have been taught that about the authority, inerrancy and infallibility of the scriptural text. They have been taught to believe that the expositor functions in a prophetic role and that he is obligated to preach the biblical text with accuracy and great care. The SBC seminaries ensure that they prepare their students to preach expository sermons and denominational leaders tend to model and adhere to the task and practice of expository preaching. Southern Seminary was initiated and served as the model for equipping students, pastors and denominational leaders to be trained practitioners of expository preaching in their local churches. It is noteworthy that the task of expository preaching involves the responsibility to ensure the fidelity of the original in the task of interpretation or translation.

Historically also, SBC expository preaching was a response to the oratory and sensationalistic preaching of the late nineteenth century. Broadus reacted to the lack of scriptural texts in sermonic presentation of his day. Broadus was critical of the use of pure rhetorical strategy to influence and lead the congregation. He considered this a disconnection between theology and preaching. He sought to ensure that sermons would be text-driven and he successfully ushered in the concept of expository preaching which was text driven accompanied by homiletics with strong contemporary appeal. Broadus's goals was to ensure that sermons was appealing, that they were text-driven or structurally developed based on the text in question and then to make practical application points or next steps for the congregation to follow. Broadus succeeded in influencing SBC seminaries, denominational leaders and future SBC leaders and pastors. The expository methodology effectively mobilized SBC congregants and moved them to act and support certain social values with understanding that they were obeying the original commands of God. SBC congregants were mobilized and roused to engage in evangelistic and missionary endeavors with the view that they were theologically motivated as the expositors functioned prophetically to convey divine commands. SBC congregants in a sense were motivated based on theological concepts and like most religious groups believed they were following actual divine truths and hence were inherently right and responsible to mobilize and obey the expository sermonic concepts.

SBC expositors were overly concerned with the theological aspects of the expository methodology but the argument for expositions seems more dependable when examined historically form the standpoint of canonicity. Canonicity refers to the idea that all sixty-six books of the Bible were recognized by the early as church as "inspired" by God who directed the human authors of the Bible to write those books using their own personalities to share the very words of God. The books of the canon were authenticated by the early church as being authoritative about Christian faith.[54]

The SBC expositor is expected interpret the Bible to render the exact words of Scriptures in their sermonic material. Since the early church viewed the text as authoritative SBC determined that they should be treated as such and that they be interpreted in their literal sense to ensure that the expositor upholds the inherent authority of text. Connected to the idea of canonicity is antiquity which simply means that the text of the Bible are all authentically written during the Old Testament times or during the first century and as such fit the criteria for being included in the canon. Again, SB pastors point to this embedded belief that the text were originally writings by OT prophets, disciples or their amanuensis and assert that the text is truly by inspired human authors. The inspired text then must be interpreted devoid of flays or any allegorical or overt spiritualization of the text. The intent of the human authors who wrote in their specific time periods must be considered and examined contextually to ensure fidelity to the text,

---

54. Gamble, "Canonical Formation," 192.

grammar and historical context. Canonicity informs the expository of not only the location of the text in the Scriptures but the historical contexts and authorial intent of the Bible writers. Connected to this is the concept of catholicity which means that the orthodox Protestant church has always accepted the sixty-six books of the Bible as authoritative, and the original manuscripts, copies, and scriptural text have been historically deemed as having value and purpose. Any misinterpretations or inaccurate renderings conflict with the standard historical rendering used to maintain orthodoxy.

The scriptural text the and the idea of a fixed canon provides the foundation for asserting that the text has historical value and has been used from the time of the early church to influence and mobilize congregations. The SBC has historically adhered to the theological concepts of inerrancy, inspiration infallibility however it is the elements of canonicity, antiquity, and catholicity that can offer a divergent perspective instead of using the text to support its own presuppositions.

Nevertheless, the task and practice of expository preaching involves a level of scholarship, the expositor has to undertake an exegetical study of the text and connect it with contemporary examples. The expository that follows this methodology can be assured that he has done the task of interpretation and has fulfilled the prophetic role and responsibility. The congregation too can be assured that their pastor is proclaim the original, unadulterated meaning which emancipates or liberates them to obey commands even if they seem archaic or traditionalistic. The SBC expositors functions with this inherent theological knowledge though predominantly circular that he is mobilizing and enabling his congregation to experience God by the only given means. The congregational response is somewhat psychological and does appeal to traditionalistic tendencies, but the undergirding issue is the self-belief in hearing God's divine voice while the translator or expositor does not create meaning but simply conveys what is already in the text.

The task of the expositor of translation, exegesis, and practical homiletics means that the expositor is relying on a message outside of himself, one that is divinely created. The words, commands and ideology are not his and so conflicts with society and culture are conflicts with God. The SBC expositor is only a mouthpiece. This understanding makes the role of the expositor ethically credible for his authority is based on his reliance on the text that must be more than a sheer perfunctory examination of the text. He is not trying to build a case for himself or for congregants to commit to God or the local church. The mechanics of exposition removes ultimate responsibility from the pastor to the congregant, and as such, the congregation must choose to obey or disobey God. The choice is subtle but significant. Every expository sermon is an intrinsic argument that God is speaking, and congregants experience tremendous psychological pressure to follow and believe. The SBC has historically used the expository model to evangelize and to teach sanctification as well as to confront societal and cultural practices that conflict with SBC values. The methodology is deeply theologically circular and entrenched in tradition and denominational history, but nonetheless it remains an effective mode for mobilizing congregants to support their local polity and disavow certain social, political, and cultural values.

Chapter 3

The Communal Role of Expository Preaching

SBC THEOLOGIANS PURPORT TO read and preach primarily based on original biblical texts to replicate the exact words of God. They assume that their reading, interpreting, and preaching are authoritative, inerrant, and infallible. SBC theologians desire to reiterate the original tone images of the biblical text for present-day Bible readers. This aspiration to garner the original meaning requires reproducing the original text for the exegetical and homiletic process and providing readers with a version of the Bible that is as close to the original as possible.

This chapter contains my analysis of the methodology of exegesis (including genre analysis) as practiced and endorsed by the foremost SBC theologians, leaders, and pastors. I describe the relationship between the exegetical and hermeneutic methodology that perpetuates SBC ideologies, as well as SBC social and political views. I anthologize the accounts of preachers and interpreters regarding their practices. Some of the central figures' writings that are discussed include Daniel Akin (president of Southeastern Seminary), David Allen (Professor of Theology and Homiletics at Southwestern Seminary), Jim Shaddix (Professor of Preaching at Southeastern Seminary), R. Albert Mohler, Jr. (President of the Southern Baptist Theological Seminary); Joseph Emerson Brown (Professor of Christian Theology). These individuals have served in SBC pulpits, on SBC higher education faculties, and well as in leadership roles in SBC seminaries. I examine their writings, sermons, and conduct interviews regarding their homiletic methodology.

Hermeneutic Methodology

The term hermeneutics is a broad classification for the process of interpreting a text based on a series of rules or interpretative laws. Grant R. Osborne asserts that "hermeneutics is a science, since it provides a logical, orderly classification of the laws of interpretation."[1] However, there is a subjective artistic aspect to the task of interpretation. Osborne argues that hermeneutics is "an art, for it is an acquired skill demanding both imagination and an ability of apply the laws to selected passages."[2] The duality of purpose and process is a symbiotic integration which involves the movement from text to the intended audience in an attempt to garner the original meaning of the text. Here the purpose is somewhat myopic in that the hermeneutical task is focused on the biblical text. The broader classification of hermeneutics is focused on all forms of text and in ontological terms its first priority is to gain an understanding of the context or specific context of the text. However, SBC theologians and modern Biblicist view the task of hermeneutics as being centered on the exegetical meaning of the text and correlating it to its significance through the contextualization and corroboration with modern culture. Therewith, there is a metaphorical spiral, from original meaning to modern author, which Osborne asserts is a better figurative means of understanding the hermeneutical process, "because it is not a closed circle but rather an open-ended movement from the horizon of the text to the horizon of the reader."

Integral to the hermeneutical process then is ascertaining the meaning of the text for the reader or audience of today. The SBC expositor aims to follow this spiraled movement and in so doing achieve the intended meaning of the text and so become empowered to authoritatively declare the original meaning of the text in a manner which makes it relevant for the reader or local church today. It is the convergence of this twofold belief that the original intended meaning has been uncovered and that it is contextually relevantly, which satiates the expectations of both the SBC expositor and SBC congregations that they are unequivocally disseminating and following religious truth. This convergence may be deemed contradictory in that the text is anchored in historical times, but a contemporary application is sought. SB theologians seek to address this by arguing that the expositor should seek to engage in an exegetical and homiletic study so that he brings the contemporary audience into an understanding of the ancient texts and to correlate similarities in the issues at hand and the prescribed meaning

---

1. Osborne, *Hermeneutical Spiral*, 5.
2. Osborne, *Hermeneutical Spiral*, 5.

for address those issues. The text retains its ancient meaning but contemporary listeners because of the exegetical methodology they can identify areas for correspondence and learning. David Dockery writes that biblical preaching is the task of bringing about an encounter between people of our times and the written Word of God, composed in another language, another time, another culture.[3] Equally important is the expression of a biblical or theological worldview in the expository sermon which enables the SBC to maintain the communal aspect of the congregation based on a set of shared values in contemporary culture.

Genre Analysis

The commitment to moving from text to contemporary significance has formed the means by which the SBC has developed and substantiated its political and social ideologies and its sense of community. Their methodology begins with an understanding of the specific genre of the texts and the appropriate interpretative schema for that genre. Genre analysis provides the means of understanding the text based on the type of literary inscription. The SBC expositor then is obligated to assess and engage in an exegetical analysis of a passage based on the rules of that genre. A general categorization of specific genres will include narrative, poetry, wisdom, prophecy, apocalyptic, parable and epistle. The literary rules that are applied to each literary grouping equips the expositor with the capacity to glean the external aspects of the texts such as its form and structure and its internal mechanisms such as the vocal pattern, narration, *Sitz im Leben* and narrative movement. The rules for each genre provide the exegetical principles for interpreting the various types of literary texts. Each grouping is comprehensively different in its form and purpose and so the interpreter is tasked with reading the text based on its historical framework and then rendering the text so that it reflects the meaning and context of the original.

The term genre here specifically refers to the different forms or literary style that the biblical writer may have used such as poetry, narrative, or even didactic prose. The identification of the specific genre aims towards preaching the text so that the literary form of the text is expressed in the sermonic moment and that the text is interpreted based on the literary grouping location of the text. This is a core tenet of expository preaching and one espoused by David Allen as against the non-traditional but mainstream homiletic approaches. Allen writes that "the New Homiletic is about: metaphor and symbol; evocation of an experience; unrestricted movement;

---

3. Dockery, "Preaching and Hermeneutics," 142.

and, of course, mystery."[4] Allen argues against the pervasiveness of narrative preaching and the approaches outlined primarily by David Buttrick and Fred Craddock. Both homileticians emphasize an experiential narrative approach to preaching. Buttrick, in his seminal work *Homiletic: Moves and Structures*, is concerned with the experience of the listeners and emphasizes the need to use imagery or contemporary illustrations to explain or give meaning to the text such as by rephrasing or explaining the text using contemporary words and images.[5] Craddock too embraces this methodology by espousing the use of images, illustrations, and contemporary examples to explain the text rather than using archaic language and ideas.

Grant Osborne addresses the importance of genre analysis in the hermeneutical process with the aim of understanding the theological meaning of the text and explained that "the place of genre in this hermeneutical process is crucial. It provides the linguistic framework for the semantic verification which the interpreter attempts."[6] Osborne argues that genre is a vital component in the expository process in that it aids in the interpretation of the biblical text. Accordingly, the interpreter can identify the genre of a biblical passage and use the rules or characteristics of the genre to interpret the text. The classificatory aspect of genre analysis allows the interpreter to use a standardize means to describe the meaning of the text. Genre analysis allows for finding the clear demarcation of form, content, purpose, and structure of the biblical text under review.

Genre analysis more pointedly does not necessarily shape the structure of the sermon but more likely informs and illumines the preacher about text structure for conveying the meaning of the text to congregants. As a part of the homiletic process, the preacher is responsible for expressing to the congregants the form of the text and for managing their expectations about how to apply, practice, and interpret the text itself. Hence, an apocalyptic text is duly expressed as such, and the preacher reminds the congregants about the futuristic tenets of the apocalyptic text. The preacher conveys communal truths, such as the eschatological return of Christ, judgment, mission of the church, and God's creation as distinctive SBC tenets. The SB theologian includes the traditional SB beliefs as intrinsic to the theological meaning of the text.

Genre analysis enables considering what the reader's response to the text may be through a focus on the inherent message of the text to uncover its main idea and connect the main idea to a sense of human consciousness

---

4. Allen, "Preaching," 62.
5. Craddock, "One Without Authority."
6. Osborne, "Genre," 1–27.

or significance. SBC theologians are keenly aware of the complexities which emanate from undertaking a genre analysis of the text. Principally, the complexities include the occurrence of mixed forms and the possibility that a text might be fused with one or more genres. The task of interpretation for the expositor then becomes somewhat tentative and problematical.

Even though the use of genre analysis is critical, the SBC expositor recognizes that it is a byproduct of the exegetical process and should be correlated with the literal interpretation of the text. Additionally, the historicity and grammatical analysis is important to attaining the literal meaning or significance of the text and takes precedent over the genre analysis. However, it is imperative for the expositor that the genre is documented and used to shape the sermon or to inform the practical application of the sermon in the homiletic process.

The genre analysis informs a correct rendering of the text; helps in conveying the meaning of the biblical text; and ascertaining the shifts in mood, tone, and point view that become apparent through the convergence of information from both literal interpretation and genre analytics. The SBC fervently supports genre analysis especially in light of its reluctance to embrace any straight, figurative reading of the text. The SBC asserts that while a text may be couched in a figurative genre or figurative speech, such as hyperbole, metaphor, or poetry, it contains concrete meaning that can be revealed through the overall exposition of its grammar, syntax, and context. According to David Allen, biblical text contains meaning at all levels in the form's genre and structure. It is the task of the interpreter to uncover any of concrete or literal meaning couched in the figurative use of speech and the form itself.[7]

Narrative Preaching

The concept of narrative preaching is based on the idea that humans do not exist deductively. Humans tend to think, dream, tell stories, watch movies, enjoy lyrics to a song, etc. Stories are an innate part of human living and the primary means of communication or sharing should not be deductive or didactic. Narrative preachers argue that since God disseminates truth in the Bible through narratives and storytellers, the contemporary sermon should take this primary form. Narrative preachers believe conveying God's word should be done in the mode of storytelling.

Narrative preachers attempt to identify the meaning of the text and to utilize contemporary stories or images for expressing the meaning of the

7. Allen, "Text-Driven Preaching."

text without overtly using biblical or theological language. However, Allen and other SBC theologians insist that sermons should take on the form of the genre and the sermon should focus on the meaning of the text without imbedding the meaning into a series of stories. Allen emphasizes the need to ensure that the primary goal of the sermon is to convey the meaning of the biblical text using the textual language and providing understanding about the meaning of the context and background of the text.

Allen refutes the narrative approach and emphasizes the need to include the aspect of genre analysis to the exegetical and exposition of the text. Allen asserts that throughout the history of church, the greatest preachers have been those who recognized that they have no authority in themselves and have seen their task as being to explain the words of Scripture and apply them clearly to the lives of their hearers. Their preaching has not drawn its power from the proclamation of their own Christian experiences or the experiences of others or from their own opinions, creative ideas, or rhetorical skills. Their preaching, declares Allen, emanates from God's powerful words. Allen argues that "those homiletes who put all their eggs in the narrative basket tend to disparage expository preaching. One finds little exposition of the text in most narrative sermons. The goal is the evocation of an experience—a very postmodern goal."[8] Allen views postmodernism as a characteristic of the current culture that is rife with relativism in which meaning remains in constant flux and uncertainty.[9] Allen is not against narrative preaching, but he is wary of the aplomb seceding of biblical text to a homiletic narrative.

The tension between expository and narrative preaching results from forcing the insertion or connection of nonbiblical texts in a sermon. Such texts do not specifically mention Jesus, may not bridge the distance between the Old and New Testament, or lack a direct connection or reference to Jesus. This practice appears irreconcilable with expository preaching because of the dictum that the text and sermon should only concentrate on the original text so any insertion violates the homiletic methodology. Moreover, the distaste for narrative preaching and its heavy reliance on storytelling is contradicted because the expository method in a sense betrays a need to invent connections between Old and New Testament.

Even though one may argue for inherent connections, it may seem that the congregational and communal expectations sometimes exceed any wholehearted commitment to be completely text centered. It is understood that Jesus Christ is the leader of the congregation. If Jesus is "speaking" in a

---

8. Allen, "Preaching" 70.
9. Allen, "Preaching" 70

biblical text, the text retains implicit authority. SBC pastors and theologians then tend to superimpose Jesus on every sermon to give the impression that Jesus is the center and voice behind the biblical text. This emphasis on Jesus as the speaker in biblical text perpetuates the willingness of SBC congregants to support SBC doctrine and dogma. Furthermore, this practice provides congregants with a sense of missional purpose for which they gather and commune.

The foundation for growth, development, and sustenance has historically been connected with the expository. But narrative preaching yields angst even though it shares the divine mandate to engage in evangelization and discipleship. The theoretical models of interpretation and application of the text form the grounds for SBC theologians, pastors, and leaders to believe that they are divinely led and supported by God. Thus, they appeal to genre, context, historicity, the original languages, syntax, and grammar as the implicit tenets of the exegetical and hermeneutical aspect of expository preaching. The SBC positional statement about the Bible states:

> The Holy Bible was written by men divinely inspired and is God's revelation of Himself to man. It is a perfect treasure of divine instruction. It has God for its author, salvation for its end, and truth, without any mixture of error, for its matter. Therefore, all Scripture is totally true and trustworthy. It reveals the principles by which God judges us, and therefore is, and will remain to the end of the world the true center of Christian union, and the supreme standard by which all human conduct, creeds, and religious opinions should be tried. All Scripture is a testimony to Christ, who is Himself the focus of divine revelation.[10]

It is not surprising that the SBC has a historical and continued commitment to the process of expository preaching. The Scripture is paramount to the SBC and foundational to the SBC's development, ethics, faith, worldview, and church community.

Expository Preaching

The goal of expository preaching is to elucidate the meaning of the ancient text and to create a sense of understanding that the congregants can embrace as a shared truth and develop obeisance due to the tenets of the biblical text. The ultimate purpose of expository preaching is to form a theologically constructed community of faith that follows the same biblical,

10. SBC, "Position Statement."

social, and cultural values. The community does not necessarily share the same experiences. However, the community develops analogous ideologies through the congregants's commitment to the theological values espoused during expository preaching. The text must be interpreted and subsequently exposited for maintaining its historically interpretative and theological origins and the values of the community.

There are tension points due to the moments when the interpretation and exposition of the text contradicts past or current SB practices. This happens when the SB church holds to values contradictory to thorough research and exposition. The issue of race is an example whereby the SB at one point encouraged segregation even though the value contradicted a canonical exposition of biblical text. Nonetheless, SB leaders see the possibility of convergence as SBC theologian Daniel L. Aikin writes about the convergence of SB theology and community values and contends that theology is based on expository preaching and the commitment to teaching the New Testament text that attracts people to the church spiritually and numerically to build a congregation. Furthermore, Aikin argues that expository preaching leads to converting people:

> The membership of the local church is made up of those who confess Christ as Savior and Lord, and whose lives give evidence of conversion. Baptist commitment to this principle set them apart from the magisterial Reformers, but they did so because of their commitment to the witness of the New Testament.[11]

Aikin, like Allen, is concerned about conserving and perpetuating SBC theology and values. Thus, they advocate for the imperative of SB congregation polity and unity through engagement with and exposition of biblical text.

This engagement with biblical text involves the process of hermeneutics including a genre analysis and homiletics that yields a logical, emotional, and ethical response. Through biblical theology and the methodology of hermeneutics espoused by the SBC, the sermon is governed by a text-driven structure to support and articulate a communal theological approach. Thomas Schriener, the James Buchanan Harrison Professor of New Testament and the Associate Dean for Scripture and Interpretation at the Southern Baptist Theological Seminary, emphasizes the importance of gleaning or identifying the meaning of the text then building the sermon to connect with the existing theological truths as believed or supported by congregants. For example, a sermon may be used to discuss relationships but should connect with the bigger theological idea of how God exists in a

---

11. Akin, "The Future," 69–71.

relationship with each person through the Trinity, referring to God, Jesus, and the Holy Spirit. This sort of preaching elevates the sermon from being merely a self-help tool to a Bible-driven experience that affirms and connects with existing theological concepts. SBC theologians fervently believe that the SBC and its local churches are not built upon or sustained by individual idea but by a collection of ideas that are distinctively SB. Shreiner asserts this belief:

> Our preaching often concentrates on steps to a successful marriage or how to raise children in our culture. Such sermons on family issues, of course, are fitting and needed. Unfortunately, two problems often surface in such sermons. First, what the Scriptures actually say about these subjects is often neglected or skated over. How many sermons on marriage faithfully and urgently set forth what Paul actually says about the roles of men and women (Eph 5:22–33)? Or, is it the case that even we conservatives are somewhat abashed and embarrassed by what the Scriptures say?
>
> The second problem is of the same sort, and perhaps even more serious. In many conservative churches pastors almost always preach on the horizontal level. The congregation is bombarded with sermons about marriage, raising children, success in business, overcoming depression, conquering fears, and so on and so forth. Again, all of these subjects must be faced in our pulpits. We must not go to the other extreme so that we never address these matters. But what is troubling is that these sort of sermons become the staple week in and week out, and the theological worldview that permeates God's word and is the foundation for all of life is passed over in silence.[12]

SB theologians, including Schreiner, believe that the hermeneutical task of preaching is not complete without engaging in or divulging some level of biblical theology. Schreiner explicated:

> Our task as preachers is to proclaim the whole counsel of God. We will not fulfill our calling if as preachers we fail to do biblical theology. We may get many compliments from our people for our moral lessons and our illustrations, but we are not faithfully serving our congregations if they do not understand how the whole of Scripture points to Christ, and if they do not gain a better understanding from us of the storyline of the Bible. May

---

12. Schreiner, "Preaching," 17.

> God help us to be faithful teachers and preachers, so that every person under our charge will be presented perfect in Christ.[13]

SB theologians and pastors focus on the need to expose the theological or biblical meaning of the text. They preach about the text itself rather than on talking points about a specific religious subject matter. In their view, understanding of the theological argument emerges from an investigation of the meaning of the biblical text's literary form, structure, and context. The need to understand the theological meaning of the text is a foremost aspect of the hermeneutical task. The beginning point for the SBC expositor is identifying the genre or literary form and then using the rules of that genre to garner the theological meaning of the text:

> Do our preachers really grasp the need to show the fruits of biblical theology in the way they preach? The only way to do this is to major on expository preaching, and in such a way that the sense of the unity of the Bible is built up. Above all, Old Testament preaching should be undertaken in a way that shows how the whole Bible testifies to Christ. Narrative should be milked first and foremost for its part in redemptive history rather than for its exemplary morals. This takes careful and time-consuming preparation.[14]

Furthermore, many SB expositors draw on the philosophical model of E. D. Hirsch, Jr., as espoused in his 1967 publication of *Validity in Interpretation*. Hirsch argues that the meaning of text is grounded in the author's intended meaning and asserts this idea as a "sensible belief."[15] Hirsch focuses on identifying the author's intended meaning and insists that failure to do so is "to reject the only compelling normative principle that [can] lend validity to an interpretation."[16] In evaluating meaning Hirsch explains as follows:

> *Meaning* is that which is represented by a text; it is what the author meant by his use of a particular sign sequence; it is what the signs represent. *Significance*, on the other hand, names a relationship between that meaning and a person, or a conception, or a situation or indeed anything imaginable.[17]

---

13. Schreiner, "Preaching," 28.
14. Schreiner, "Preaching," 17.
15. Hirsch, *Validity in Interpretation*, 1.
16. Hirsch, *Validity in Interpretation*, 5.
17. Hirsch, *Validity in Interpretation*, 8.

Hirsch states that one can garner the intended meaning of a text as "an entity which is self-identical . . . which always remains the same from one moment to the next—that it is changeless."[18] Hirsch also defines meaning "as a *willed type* which an author expresses by linguistic symbols and which can be understood by another through those symbols."[19] For Hirsch, there is a semblance or interchangeability and reproducibility of the author's intended meaning. Hirsch discusses genre "which embraces the whole meaning of an utterance."[20] He asserts that the interpreter "must master not only the variable and unstable norms of language but also the particular norms of a particular genre."[21] Hirsch posits that through a study of the genre "that sense of the whole by means of which an interpreter can correctly understand any part in its determinacy."[22]

Hirsch allows that the genre is not always acquiescent with the meaning of text it is a methodology for unearthing the intended meaning of text: "We may now say that the implications of an utterance are determined by its intrinsic genre. The principle by which we can discover whether an implication belongs to a meaning turns out to be the concept of intrinsic genre."[23] Therefore, a specific interpretation of a text can be considered valid if the interpretation follows the mode of the genre and its associated rules or conventions.

David Allen and Jerry Vines, two SBC stalwarts, emphasize the necessity of this threefold process which includes the possibility of genre of analysis all in an effort to garner the original meaning of the text and ensure its applicable and appropriate communication:

> Hermeneutics, exegesis, and proclamation form the crucial triad with which every pastor must reckon. A proper biblical hermeneutic provides the philosophical underpinnings which undergird the exegetical task. Likewise, a proper exegetical methodology provides the foundation for the sermon. Then, of course, proper sermon delivery is necessary to carry home God's truth to the hearer.[24]

Vines and Allen connect between Hirsch's viewpoint and the task of hermeneutics:

18. Hirsch, *Validity in Interpretation*, 46.
19. Hirsch, *Validity in Interpretation*, 49.
20. Hirsch, *Validity in Interpretation*, 71.
21. Hirsch, *Validity in Interpretation*, 71.
22. Hirsch, *Validity in Interpretation*, 86.
23. Hirsch, *Validity in Interpretation*, 89–90.
24. Vines and Allen, "Hermeneutics, Exegesis, and Proclamation," 309.

> Hirsch's categories of "meaning" and "significance" are important and helpful for us. When the biblical exegete comes to a text of Scripture, he can proceed on the premise that there is a determinate meaning there. His job is to discover this meaning through exegesis. Having done this, there remains the further task of applying this meaning to modern day man.[25]

The SBC expositor has a responsibility to develop text-driven sermons inclusive of the necessity for genre analysis as part of the methodology for extricating the original meaning of the text. In genre analysis, there is a level of reciprocity between reader and the biblical text. The reader is able to connect particular genres's characteristics with the biblical text. One scholar calls this *genre competence* as it "designates a potential of human beings for understanding presently existing and future possible texts, given that such texts are structured according to specifiable genre principles."[26] Accordingly, once the genre is examined and understood, the theological or biblical meaning becomes apparent leading to the textual connection with distinctive SBC ideals. The text essentially serves as a communal or congregational force.

SBC congregants hear sermons not only about a text dealing with a personal subject matter or issue at hand but also about calls for all of them to support an overarching theological and social agenda. SBC congregants have the opportunity to react or respond both to personal tensions and to conjoined together for supporting or fighting a common cause. The simple and sublime effect of SBC preaching is the clear theological truths that will be apparent in SBC sermons. These truths fall under a larger category of theological ideas that serve as SBC distinctives. It is these distinctive ideas that form the SBC theological identity and hence their sermonic materials uphold and support these ideas and form the basis of community beliefs.

SBC theologians and pastors understand their interpretation and preaching of biblical texts shape the characters and mindsets of SBC adherents. Akin explains:

> World Christians recognize that they are citizens of a different kind of nation, a different kind of kingdom, a different kind of community. And yet, they also recognize that they live in this world as well, a world that is not their home, but one in which they serve as a royal ambassadors fulfilling the ministry of reconciliation (2 Cor. 5:18–21). They are here as divine representatives to call men and women from this world kingdom

---

25. Vines and Allen, "Hermeneutics, Exegesis, and Proclamation," 309.
26. Gerhart, "Generic Competence," 32.

into God's glorious kingdom. This assignment calls for *wisdom* and *winsomeness*. It calls for conviction as well as compassion. It requires that we plant our feet in the *Scriptures* while keeping a watchful and discerning eye on the *culture*.[27]

SB theologians and pastors connect with and grow their congregations based on focused expository preaching which teaches Scripture and develops communities built upon shared beliefs. SBC leaders note they have the largest Protestant denomination in the United States as a result of their focus on expository preaching and its ability to build and galvanize people around shared beliefs. Accordingly, SBC consists of 47,272 churches with a total membership of about 15.2 million congregants. Weekly attendance at worship services is about 5.2 million worshipers. SBC leaders oversee an extensive missionary program throughout the U.S. and abroad and operates six seminaries with a total enrollment of more than twenty one thousand students.

In essence, the SBC community which is comprised of individual congregations locate their unity and cohesiveness in the Scriptures. However, they do not purport a superficial understanding of various texts or simply ritualize a tradition to create and maintain unity. It is a commitment to studying the text through a careful exegetical methodology and to remaining cognizant of the historical context and linguistic domain of the text.

The goal is to unsheathe the original meaning for SBC congregants and all congregations to ensure they hear the same original message as delivered by the historical writers, prophets, and Jesus himself. For the SBC, the original words of the Bible are divine and lifegiving. This mystical understanding of the Bible's text makes it the center of the local church and the harbinger of truth. SBC theologians in a very concentric way have built a theology of the Bible in which the text is divine and empowering and used to form and maintain community. The SB pastor's and theologian's chief responsibility involves teaching the exact meaning of biblical text to community that can be informed and galvanized around these intrinsic truths.

A typical SBC congregant serves as the recipient of a sermon based on the original meaning of the text. Because of this dynamic, SB sermons as derived from the text with the expository method communicate the same message to all congregants and churches over many centuries. Furthermore, since the SBC has a set of systematic doctrines or beliefs and these too have been communicated in sermons, SBC congregations typically hear the same doctrines and the same core tenets from every biblical text. This uniformity occurs on two levels.

---

27. Gerhart, "Generic Competence," 32

Firstly, through the expository methodology represents a codified, rigorous, and somewhat scientific process used by all SBC pastors and theologians to glean the core tenets or meanings from every text or passage of Scripture. The expository methodology not only contributes to the garnering of similar beliefs through its codified process of examining and revealing the meaning of the text but also ensures the protection of SB doctrinal stances. The uniformity on this first level is propagated in SB seminaries and publishing companies. The outcome yields uniformity of methodology by theologians and pastors at SB seminaries to ensure all present and future pastors become committed to the same belief and methodology.

Secondly, in a very antiquated way, Biblical meaning is in a fixed state for the SBC. The SBC exegetical methodology is thoroughly focused on investigating the original text so that over time the expository task produces the recurring meanings that form the SBC's historical and traditional beliefs. These in turn become imbedded in family structures, in SB communities, and across generations. This simple consternation with meaning creates within local SBC communities a subculture guided by SBC doctrines that usually fall within the scope of conservative values. This subculture is historically conservative and overtly biblical. Consequently, generations of families and entire communities subscribe to and identify with SBC beliefs. What makes this subculture uniquely interesting is that SBC congregants then have a both uniquely religious but also political and social form of unity. Thus, the communal aspect is deep (historical and tradition) and wide (generational and social).

Furthermore, the SBC's doctrinal beliefs and textual rendering foster a sense in which the local congregation and convention in general preserve biblical and national history, culture, and values. The SBC inherently believes that the prosperity and wellbeing of the United States is due to its citizens's and residents's overall commitment to God and the Bible. Hence, the national values and biblical values are assumed to ensure God's continued blessing upon the nation. SBC congregants maintain a sense of obligation for obeying and teaching these tenets to the forthcoming generations. While there are no overt claims that the commands of the Bible should be embraced nationally, the SBC promotes the connection between the holy lands of Israel and the local church communities, both of which have experienced God's presence and help when the people obey biblical guidance.[28]

The potency of expository preaching in light of congregational obeisance creates both a demand for its continued practice and an undying commitment to its practice. SB expository practitioners come to their

---

28. SBC, "Basic Beliefs."

congregations who share an underlying belief that these pastors have researched and studied artistically and scientifically the original text to garner the original meaning of the original text. The congregants can be assured about hearing the original, divine ordinances and the pastor can be trusted with expositional sermon delivery. Additionally, there is an expectation that SBC pastors and theologians can show evidence of exegetical study when opening the Bible. This means that the sermon contains evidence of being written in antiquity (i.e., prehistoric times). However, the text is explained using contemporary illustrations and applications. The innate congregational acceptance of the sermon studied exegetically couples with the belief in the pastor showing how the biblical text's contemporary application leads to a demand for its continued practice.

Congregations expect to hear about a historically divine ordinance which should be applied in contemporary times. Every congregation receives similar sermons with equivalent core tenets weekly. SBC congregations gather to hear the weekly divine directive in hopes that they will continue to experience divine blessings or preferential treatment from God. The process of communicating the text becomes increasingly important so as to ensure that the ancient text is expressed and corroborated in both contemporary language and illustrations.

Homiletic Methodology

A close examination of the hermeneutic and homiletic methodology of the leading SBC preachers, professors, and seminary administrators indicates a commitment to the expository methodology of preaching. Accordingly, Daniel Akin writes about the importance of exposition and the exclusive utilization of the texts of Scripture to inform, instruct, and influence the SBC:

> Seduced by the sirens of modernity we have jettisoned a word-based ministry that is expository in nature. We have, in our attempt to be popular and relevant, become foolish and irrelevant. Skiing across the surface needs of a fallen, sinful humanity we have turned the pulpit into a pop-psychology side-show and a feel-good pitstop. We have neglected preaching the whole counsel of God's Word and the theology of God's Word. Too many of our people know neither the content of Scripture or the doctrines of Scripture. Preaching the cross of Christ and the bloody atonement accomplished by His death is the exception rather than the norm. Some choose to focus on politics, others the emotions, still others relationships and the list goes on and

on. If the Bible is used at all, it is usually as a proof-text out of context with no real connection to what the speaker is saying.[29]

Akins laments the incursion of liberal theologies in modern day pulpits:

> Practically, the various liberal theologies orbiting about us have their own particular and peculiar interest. Starting, almost always, with their experience and situatedness, their agendas are driven by personal, social and cultural concerns. On those occasions when The Bible can be summoned for support, they will allow the Scripture to make a brief appearance. Once its usefulness has been served, it is dismissed from the playing field and sent back to the sidelines where it spends most of its time.[30]

Akin decries the lack of exposition and calls for a more potent use of Scripture against the current languid, anemic approaches which he identified. He assesses the spiritual strata as ineffective and that much of contemporary preaching is devoid of an expository methodology. Akin, asserts:

> Claiming to believe in an infallible and inerrant Bible (though some are now questioning this), and affirming that it is alive and powerful, they nonetheless handle it in a way that, in my mind, raises serious questions of theological integrity and spiritual wisdom. In terms of theological integrity such preaching betrays its convictions, at least methodologically. In the context of spiritual wisdom, it says we can see people converted and brought to maturity in Christ without the consistent teaching of the whole counsel of God's Word. Further, at least implicitly, it questions the judgment of God the Holy Spirit in inspiring Scripture to be written as we have it. Topical preaching, narrative preaching, emerging preaching, and yes, even some types of doctrinal preaching, fundamentally suggest by their method and practice that the Holy Spirit should have packaged The Bible differently. This is spiritually ignorant at best, and arrogant at worst.[31]

Akin believes there is an overwhelming need for expository preaching, even though he admits that there is a tendency for applying poor homiletic methodology. Akin argues for expository preaching that is engaging as acutely important. Akin noted that:

> Some evangelicals have argued that biblical exposition cannot reach the twenty-first century believer. Others have criticized

29. Akin, "Chapel Message, October 19, 2005."
30. Akin, "Mullins Lectures, October 5, 2005."
31. Akin, "Mullins Lectures, October 5, 2005."

exposition saying it is dull and boring, dry, uninspiring and irrelevant. These kinds of criticisms are legitimate if you are critiquing "bad preaching." However, these barbs are out of bounds if engaging exposition is the target. I am convinced that the need for preaching that is faithful and inspiring, expository and engaging has never been greater.[32]

Akin defines expository preaching as follows:

> Text driven preaching that honors the truth of Scripture as it was given by the Holy Spirit. Discovering the God-inspired meaning through historical-grammatical-theological investigation and interpretation, the preacher, by means of engaging and compelling proclamation, explains, illustrates and applies the meaning of the biblical text in submission to and in the power of the Holy Spirit, preaching for a verdict of changed lives.[33]

Akin includes both the purpose and process for preaching and believes that this methodology is vital for any good practice of preaching. Akin notes that the text should form and drive the structure of the sermon and shape the final homiletic outcome "as it relates to the explanation of the biblical text."[34] Akin undoubtedly subscribes to the principle of authorial intent as he claims:

> The faithful expositor is humbled, even haunted, by the realization that when he stands to preach he stands to preach what has been given by the Holy Spirit of God. Why is he haunted? Because he understands that what is before his eyes is divinely inspired by God, and he trembles at the very thought of abusing, neglecting or altering what God Himself wrote. Yes, the Bible is best described as the Word of God written in the words of men. However, it is ultimately the Word of God, and the divine author's intended meaning as deposited in the text should be honored."[35]

Akin's belief in the divine efficacy of the Bible appears in his unwavering commitment to the theological idea about the preaching moment when he delivers the very words of God to the congregants. Furthermore, Akin alludes to the need for engaging preaching through the use of illustrations and practical action steps for the congregants because he sees illustrations as windows to help the congregants see clearly the biblical meaning behind

32. Akin, "Mullins Lectures, October 5, 2005."
33. Akin, "Mullins Lectures, October 5, 2005."
34. Akin, "Mullins Lectures, October 5, 2005."
35. Akin, "Mullins Lectures, October 5, 2005."

the sermon. The congregants achieve clarity, touched hearts, empathy, and examples of biblical works in daily living. Biblical illustrations should be focused only on proclamations by Jesus, "the master illustrator [of] the action that needs to take place on the part of the audience that should result from the message."[36]

Expository Preaching and Southern Baptists's Social Conservatism

Akin undoubtedly promotes the expository sermon as not only theologically accurate but also practically relevant. Akin underscores the ultimate outcome of biblical preaching or expository preaching as influencing the congregation to engage or fulfil the mandates of the Scripture. He believes that the sermon is not complete until a call to action or a move to ensure that the congregants obey or follow the directives of the text whether prescriptive or descriptive is conveyed. Akin is devoted to a form of text-driven biblical theology in which the text drives the theological ideas of each passage or sermon. Akin assumes that by allowing the text driven approach to form the theological idea of the text, the expositor avoids superimposing subjective, prevailing, and traditional theological values.

Akin attempts to derive a text driven exposition of each passage to uncover the inherent theological ideas that correspond with core SBC theological tenets. Each passage or sermon elucidates the voice and exaltation of Jesus Christ or encourages the readers to respond to Jesus Christ through obedient allegiance. It follows then that any approach to preaching which intrinsically underscores a commitment to Jesus Christ has a traditional, conservative following of adherents. SBC culture is innately mission oriented and acutely evangelistic and values an approach that elevates the person of Jesus. This causes its adherents to believe that they are fulfilling a divine mission whenever they obey the practical portions of expository preaching.

Akin along with SBC theologians and pastors expect to preach a sermon based solely on a specific biblical text. The goal of the sermon involves explaining the text and providing practical steps for congregants to take based on what the text alludes to. However, intrinsic to the sermon, regardless of where it is located in the Bible, is showing the biblical connection with Jesus Christ. Since SBC congregants's ultimate loyalty lies with Jesus, the expositor is tasked to revealed or connect with some aspect of the person or character of Jesus in every sermon. This effort proves to the congregation

---

36. Akin, "Mullins Lectures, October 5, 2005."

that the expositor is faithful to the expository methodology and maintains the communal aspect of shared beliefs.

It is apparent that for SB theologians and pastors, the sermon and congregation exist in a symbiotic relationship in that the sermon serves as the vehicle for communicating life-change but also ensuring that the entire community hears and advocates the same theological ideas and message. It is the doctrinal content of the sermon and its application thereon which ensure that the fabric of the community remains unequivocally or disjunctively Southern Baptist in its values. Akin further develops the contrast between a truly Christian community, which is Southern Baptist, and the culture in general. Accordingly, for SB theologians and pastors, there is a clear demarcation between the values of the SBC and the typical citizenry. Akin connects the preaching, doctrine and values and argues for a characteristically SBC theologically flora. Akin develops this contrast and argues for distinguishable ecclesiological physiognomies between contemporary values and the SBC:

> World Christians recognize that they are citizens of a different kind of nation, a different kind of kingdom, a different kind of community. And yet, they also recognize that they live in this world as well, a world that is not their home, but one in which they serve as a royal ambassadorsfulfilling the ministry of reconciliation (2 Cor. 5:18–21). They are here as divine representativesto call men and women from this world kingdom into God's glorious kingdom. This assignment calls for wisdom and winsomeness. It calls for conviction as well as compassion. It requires that we plant our feet in the Scriptures while keeping a watchful and discerning eye on the culture.How can we live out this calling to be God's people in God's world? I want to provide or us a biblically based strategy for faithfully accomplishing this assignment, one that is transferable to any cultural context whether in North America or around the world. There are biblical principles that are true anywhere, anytime, and under any circumstances that will help us communicate and "live out" the gospel more clearly. A great place to discover this strategy is found in 1 Corinthians. Here was a church gone wild, a church in a titanic battle in terms of its moral and ethical decision-making. They were struggling, and struggling mightily, both inside and outside their community, and they had the awesome task of being the Church in a radically secular, immoral, non-Christian context. Maintaining a clear gospel witness was difficult and problematic. Therefore, Paul wrote this letter in order to instruct the Corinthians in how to live out a gospel-centered

ethic. Within 1 Corinthians 6:12–13:13, he sets forth a number of universal, non-negotiable principles that would enable them to engage the culture with integrity while staying true to the gospel of Jesus Christ both in what they said and how they lived.[37]

SBC pastors and theologians practice the art and science of preaching to ensure they are authentic in their study and examinations of the original text using all the techniques and methodologies for understanding the original form and genre of the text. SBC pastors and theologians make certain that the biblical exposition is true to the text and trusted by congregants. The expositor's willingness to ensure that the sermon focuses only on the text being examined is critical, and the expositional sermon always ensures that SBC doctrine and dogma is communicated and upheld. The sermon represents an ongoing expression of the SBC values and traditions rooted in ancient biblical texts and almost impenetrable to doubt or scrutiny. The major argument against expository sermonizing could be the reliance that SBC pastors have about ancient principles that are not warranted or necessary today, or are just simply outdated.

However, the fact that the sermonic material garnered from the text continues to represent the divine conditions for communal existence, blessings, and prosperity leads SBC pastors and theologians to be adversely opposed to any other form of preaching. The exegetical methodology and homiletic exposition of the Bible reinforces SB theologians's and pastors's beliefs in the accuracy of their preaching as a truthful rendering of the text, as if God were speaking directly to the congregants. When a congregant, entire congregation, and denomination believes that God is speaking directly to the congregants during the sermon and that history and tradition are on the seller's side as is the case with SB (traditionally in Southern States) then community and values are both built and maintained through the preaching. In other words, the foundation of the SBC was centered on doctrine and dogma which came through exposition. SB theologians and pastors believe that the continued growth of the community can only be maintained by the commitment to expository preaching. Dr. Akin references the SBC's historical struggle between its moderate and conservative arms as affecting the effaceable need to enforce and uphold the expository methodology:[38]

> Southern Baptists have a hopeful future if they continually make clear their commitment to the inerrant and infallible Word of

---

37. Dr. Akin addresses ten foundational questions for ethical decision-making and applies them to the issue of alcohol abstinence in, "Emerging Church and Ethical Choices."

38. Akin, "Southern Baptists, Evangelical."

God affirming its sufficiency in all matters. (Matt 5:17–18; John 10:35; 17:17; 2 Tim 3:16–17; 2 Peter 1:20–21). Southern Baptists won the "battle for the Bible" that began in 1979. Men of God like Jimmy Draper, Paige Patterson, Paul Pressler, Adrian Rogers, and Jerry Vines put it all on the line because they saw what the poison of liberalism was doing to our Convention and its institutions. These men are heroes of the faith and what they did must be honored and never forgotten. We must keep on reminding a new generation of what happened when they were small or not yet born. It is easy for young Southern Baptists to forget Joseph, to forget the sacrifices of their fathers. However, the "war for the Bible" is not over and it will never end until Jesus returns. The war over the truthfulness of God's word was launched in the Garden of Eden when Satan asked, "Has God said?" The Word of God will continue to be under assault, and we must ever be on guard and ready to answer those who question its veracity and accuracy. A younger generation of Southern Baptists will face this challenge, and they must be warned not to squander away precious theological ground that is absolutely essential to a healthy and hopeful future for this convention of churches. Dr. Russ Bush who is now with our Lord was absolutely correct. I heard him say in a seminary classroom in the early 1980s that "the question of biblical inspiration is ultimately a question of Christological identity." Why? Because Jesus believed the Holy Scriptures to be the completely true and trustworthy Word of God! Even Rudolf Bultmann said this about our Lord, he just believes Jesus got it wrong! To deny inerrancy is to say that Jesus was wrong or that He willfully deceived. That is both heresy and blasphemy. It is spiritually suicidal! Do you doubt or deny the full truthfulness of the Bible? My counsel is go and join another denomination. We will love you and pray for you, but we do not want you infecting our people with a spiritual disease that is always fatal to the Church of the Lord Jesus. Inerrancy and the sufficiency of the Bible in all matters of faith and practice must never be up for debate in the Southern Baptist Convention.

Most important for Akin and the SBC is the discipleship of the congregants, the conversion of the masses, and the rejuvenation of the entire convention. The SB convention is known for its Sunday school classes format and focus on baptism. On Sundays, groups of congregants meet to study the Bible in condensed preaching moments that include the exposition of text and the study of a biblical topic. During these Bible studies, congregants read, reflect, and ask questions about the biblical text or topic. Undoubtedly, these preaching moments fall under the concept of discipleship wherein congregants learn SB doctrine and dogma. They engage in apologetic evangelism and become equipped to know how to respond to societal norms or cultural ideas that contradict SB values, equipping them to influence and convert others to SB ideology. This concern with conversion and baptism is typical of SB hermeneutics and eschatology and is supremely important to their practice of expository preaching. There is a belief that every individual has an eternal destiny. Thus, the church must preach only what God proclaims, since Jesus is responsible for all eternal outcomes as revealed in the Bible. Akin's perspective is the following:

> We are all going to go somewhere when we die. Death is not the end. We are either going to heaven or hell. We are going to spend eternity with a gracious and glorious God or with the evil one the Bible calls Satan or the Devil. For Christians, there is no doubt or debate about which way we are going."[39]

SB theologians argue that only the Bible explains and details the expectations that God has for human beings hence all the more reason to engage in the full-proof methodology of expository preaching. Of note, an essential belief imbued in the practice of expository preaching purports that because of the exegesis of the original text which took into account the form, semantical domain, genre, and historical contexts of the original text, the expository sermon is accurate and upholds the infallibility of the original. The exegetical study and expository sermon establish the accurate rendering and discourse of the original text and can be trusted. SBC pastors and theologians argue that every sermon's content can be trusted and that text that seems questionable still upholds divine ordinances because it comes from a higher source or power even though it may clash with personal experience. The conflict is not in the text but between human and divine understanding, because human beings are limited in their beliefs. This approach seems overtly simplistic on the part of SB theologians and pastors and eschews responsibility to the listener of the sermon and not necessarily on the expositor to prove the sermon's point. The stance involves believing that doubt or fear can be avoided if one places full and complete trust in biblical text.

Extremely important to the concept of expository is the idea of obeisance and the rewards for doing so. An exposition of the Old Testament will reveal that there are individual and communal rewards for obedience to God, as was the case with Israel. The idea here is that Israel was God's

---

39. Akin, "Acts 1–11 Conference, November 13, 2009."

chosen nation and so God has an eternal covenant or concern with its welfare. It is not surprising that the SBC, because of their understanding of the Old Testament and God's relationship with Israel, sees a pivotal role for Israel and a primary concern that the United States of America and its partners must protect and support Israel. Akin states, "Israel, the people with whom God made an eternal covenant, becomes prominent and the focal point of much that occurs at the end of the age (Rom 11; Rev 7)."[40] Akin argues regarding recent history:

> We have to acknowledge that the return of the Jews to the land of Israel changed everything in terms of perspective for many concerning particular texts of Scripture. An example would be Romans 11:25–26, where the Bible says there is coming a day when all Israel will be saved. We must not spiritualize this text into being the church. We believe it to be Israel. . .you begin to understand that God is not finished with the Jewish people and plans to use them in an extraordinary way as we move toward the end of the age.[41]

Broadly speaking, the SBC has an overarching commitment to Jewish nationalism; the evangelism of the Jews; and the social, political, and economic interests of Israel. Akin and SB leaders consistently support the interests of Israel and not just as a simplistic acquiescence to its needs as a nation. The commitment is due to the eschatological hermeneutic methodology as seen in their expositional efforts and their continued advocacy for Israel. Like Israel, the individual Christian, church community, and SBC experiences earthly benefits and rewards by obeying and supporting divine mandates that include observing God's covenant with Israel. Hence, the commitment to preaching Old Testament texts in their proper context shows how God addressed Israel and the how God will deal with communities that follow the Bible. The common thread is that expository preaching and SB congregants accept that there are divine rewards for congregations that are obedient to God and loyal to Israel. Consequently, SB congregations expect to be divinely rewarded in the present and future, like Israel, when they obey God's directions in biblical text and support of the nation of Israel.

The SBC exegetical and theological methodology evidenced in SB preaching creates a community of characteristically social conservatives who share the message as attractional in its appeal to individuals with traditional social values. The essence of expository preaching involves propagating meaning that is conservative by any social standard because the

40. Akin, "Acts 1–11 Conference, November 13, 2009."
41. Akin, "Acts 1–11 Conference, November 13, 2009."

historicity of the connection between faith and rewards for the community is built on a premise that socially conservative values equate biblical values. Expository preaching emphasizes socially conservative values and demands that SB followers practice these principles as embedded in the text. The social values articulated by SB pastors and theologians encompass several social issues such as their stance on abortion, alcohol, gambling, marriage, immigration, divorce, and separation of church and state. These are issues that are not necessarily foundational doctrinal beliefs but are unique identifiers and motivators for galvanizing the local SBC churches and the convention at large. These values have become dogma and denote what it means to follow SBC doctrine, both historically and in the present.

The SB church has been motivated not only by its commitment to a literal interpretation but to a fear arising out of this interpretative methodology. SB theologians and pastors see themselves as preservers of society who ensure that society reflects the values found in their biblical beliefs and stances. On one level, SB theologians, pastors, and leaders argue that as society becomes increasingly antibiblical, it will experience the wrath of God. The resultant effects of God's wrath will negatively impact the church and its surrounding communities. Even though SBC church leaders want to maintain a somewhat idealist societal experience based solely on biblical standards, they practice shielding, protecting, and positively impacting society according to their own biblical standards. This practice represents the move from pure adherence to foundational doctrine that requires a broader approach to impacting society. SB pastors and theologians use the expository methodology to represent a deep and sincere concern with the beneficent welfare of society in general.[42]

The issues that SB theologians and pastors advocate have become paramount because their stance was developed based on expository analysis and preaching of various texts. Hence a textual consideration has been elevated to foundational dogma because of the insistence that all texts are equally inspired and should be followed albeit in somewhat of a selective manner depending of the cultural climate and the extent to which SBC churches's leaders believe that their communities or all of society are at risk so they advocate for their biblical stance. Expository preaching in SB contexts gives credence to dogmatic stances because of the inherent belief that the issue being addressed has been addressed by God in the Bible.

This penchant for embracing and propagating social conservative values extends to the political area because of the Republican Party's tendency

---

42. Lischer, "Sermon on the Mount," 157–69; Blomberg, "How the Church Can Turn," 10–12.

to support socially conservative ideologies. For example, the SB church supports the Tea Party arm of the Republican Party. Richard Land, former president of the ethics and religious commission within the SB church comments on the Tea Party Movement:

> Indiana governor and likely Republican presidential candidate Mitch Daniels has suggested that Americans call a "truce" on divisive social issues until our precarious financial house is back in order. Many pundits have praised the idea, typically thrilled that a Republican leader seems willing to jettison, even temporarily, strong positions on abortion or gay marriage. But social conservatives are mad, and rightly so. Throughout the 1980s and '90s, social conservatives were the foot soldiers for Republican victories—only to see their issues bargained away or shoved to the bottom of the GOP agenda, beneath issues of fiscal and foreign policy. Reacting to Gov. Daniels, former Arkansas governor and presidential candidate Mike Huckabee recently said: "For those of us who have labored long and hard in the fight to educate the Democrats, voters, the media and even some Republicans on the importance of strong families, traditional marriage and life to our society, this is absolutely heartbreaking." Perhaps Gov. Daniels interprets the emergence of the tea party as a sign that GOP candidates don't have to depend on social-issues voters as they once did. That seems unlikely. As Tony Perkins of the Family Research Council has said, "Calling for a truce on core conservative principles might get you some high profile media sound bites, but it won't win you the Republican presidential nomination." Consider recent polls from the Pew Research Center's Forum on Religion & Public Life and the Public Religion Research Institute (PRRI). They reveal that tea party supporters, while motivated by the fiscal crisis, are also overwhelmingly socially conservative: Sixty-three percent oppose abortion, found PRRI, and 64% oppose same-sex marriage, found Pew. PRRI also found that 22% of voters identify with "the conservative Christian movement" but only 11% identify with the tea party. This dovetails nicely with the fact that 32% of voters in the 2010 election described themselves in exit polls as pro-life, pro-family conservatives. They voted 78% for Republican candidates, delivering House Republicans their new majority. . . ..For Republicans to do anything to de-energize this voting bloc would amount to political suicide. There is a deep longing in large segments of the American populace for a restoration of a morality that emphasizes personal obligations and responsibilities over rights and privileges. Such a society

will have a restored moral symmetry in which exemplary personal and professional behavior is rewarded and less exemplary behavior is not. As Jesus reminded us, "Man shall not live on bread alone."[43]

It is apparent that there is an inference that SBC dogma and doctrine purport high moral standards and values to maintain stability and positive morality in society. The core of this idea emerges from the belief that SB theologians and pastors interpret biblical text for conveying truthful ideologies. Essentially, if these ideologies are followed, the SBC's congregants and leaders will preserve and protect society from degradation and God's wrathful vengeance. As Land mentioned, the idea requires following Jesus leads to depending and relying on God who gives life, blessings, and prosperity. Interestingly, Land connects between social conservativism and spiritual attunement. It is clear the that Land and SB theologians in general embrace conservative ideology, such as that of the Tea Party Movement in U.S. politics, because it represents the communal aspect of SB dogma in which congregants gather and commit to certain social values. This connection is founded on the outcome of the exegetical methodology. SB traditional dogma involves serving as the preserver and protector of modern cultural values. The communal aspect of shared social conservative values results in the SBC appearing to support Republican party candidates in the U.S. Yes, the clear demarcation or denunciation of President Trump's outspoken criticism of immigrants and berating of public officials has happened, but the fact remains that his policies have been supported by SBC leaders and pastors, such as from the pulpit of FBC Dallas by Jeffress who has long been considered the most conservative standard bearer for SB tradition.

SB pastors and churches have used their expository methodology and communal commitment to certain dogma and doctrine to align their biblical expositions with Republican ideologies. SB pastors have supported Republican candidates as well as the current President. Even though SB theologians, pastors, and leaders have supported Republican ideals due to their believing the Republican Party will protect and uphold some of the biblical values they espouse, contradictions have happened within the SB community, namely the prioritizing of people, specifically loving people, as a biblical mandate. Loving people is the most important mandate based on an exegesis and exposition of the Bible.

The care for immigrants appears in Old Testament theology, but the Republican Party and current White House have violated this principle many times by belittling immigrants and publicly shaming people who

---

43. Land, "Americans Don't Want."

oppose or disagree with Republican policies. The association with the Republican Party and President has created a sense of distrust of not only in the SBC but also in other religious institutions. If SBC theologians who claim to be adept at accurate exegetical analysis and expository preaching can circumvent clear biblical commands to pursue influential partnerships with the government, then the denomination should not be trusted. The mainstay of the partnership with the Republican Party and with presidential politics indicates efforts to preserve community and ultimately to influence the judicial and executive branches of U.S. government. SB leaders, in essence, believe they can win the culture war if the Supreme Court has a majority of socially conservative judges who will possibly or potentially reverse decisions or will block any laws that violate SB communal beliefs or deviate from socially conservative Bible-based values.

SBC leaders seem to have compromised their doctrine and dogma by pursuing certain doctrines and policies as priorities because of what they consider to be extremely negative ramifications on society. There are conservative voices, such as Paige Patterson, who support the care of immigrants.[44] However, Patterson himself has been removed, or dethroned, as one of the primary SBC leaders because he suppressed evidence about the rape of a student as President of the Southwestern Baptist Theological Seminary.[45] Hence, even though they claim to accurately interpret and proclaim the biblical text and argue that their community is founded and sustained by their commitment to these doctrines, SBC leaders have demonstrated clear inconsistencies in following their own interpretative schema.

There is an apparent ongoing tension between SB belief and practice. This tension is not only seen in SB leadership lapses or affiliation with the Republican Party but also in SB leaders's actions regarding other core social issues. For example, SBC leaders support racial reconciliation, educational reform, and environmental policies based on their assumptive theological and expository approach. In 1995, the SBC drafted a resolution apologizing for their support and engagement in slavery and for their inept efforts at developing a proper relationship with African Americans. SBC leaders sought to address the burgeoning complexity in their relationship with other racial groups.[46]

The 1995 policy statement was not the first time for this issue to be part of the SBC's agenda. In June 5, 1968, the messengers not only approved "A

---

44. Ethics and Religious Liberty Commission of the Southern Baptist Convention, "SBC's Paige Patterson Calls for Immigration Reform."

45. Roach, "Patterson Denies."

46. Southern Baptist Convention.Net, "Resolution on Racial Reconciliation."

Statement Concerning the Crisis in Our Nation," confessing their share of responsibility for inadequately influencing the "conditions in which justice, order, and righteousness can prevail," but also elected W. A. Criswell as the convention's president.[47] Criswell's election was unexpected because of his previous tirade and his segregationist stance. Criswell said, "I have enlarged my sympathies and my heart during the past few years," and the church's doors are open to anyone who comes inside with sincerity.[48] Criswell, long considered an artful expositor, had interpreted and preached that Blacks were an inferior race based on his exegesis and homiletic approach to Genesis 9:20–27. Criswell surmised that African Americans inherited not Noah's curse, but God's curse, as "a servant people." Invoking the image of the Hamite curse, Criswell sought to influence his congregation and other converts about the racial incongruity between Blacks and Whites for years. Criswell elevated Whites and advocated a view that placed supreme emphasis on Whites. It is interesting that Criswell utilized an exposition of Revelation's Chapter 3 to elucidate his changed view on race relations and segregation. A copy of the 1968 sermon he preached to his church indicates no true exegesis of the text, and ironically, Criswell admitted as much. This transformation of ideologies which came at the point when he assumed the presidency of the SBC suggests political shenanigans, or at the very least, a convenient change of heart in order to solidify the presidency and nomination.[49]

It is somewhat astonishing that this foremost expositor would make a gargantuan about-face without applying his commitment to Biblicism or the expository hermeneutic. Criswell and his mentee Patterson both made crucial, homiletic contradictions. These contradictions resulted from abandonment or oversight of their own exegetical methodology. It seems that on some occasions their methodology would have yielded a certain interpretation but their choice to ignore or abandon the full use of the expositional methodology resulted in a stance that deviated from SB traditional communal beliefs. In this case, Criswell made an interpretative stance on social and church politics. One could say he decided to embrace racial equality and desegregation in order to assume the presidency of the convention. Criswell was also under social pressure to comply with societal changes, and the congregation was willing to accept the change, so Criswell complied. The case of Criswell displays how expository hermeneutics can submit to communal pressures devoid of biblical exegesis when the stance reflects social conservative values. This submission to society's values is a clear danger for SBC

---

47. *Annual of the Southern Baptist Convention*, 1968.
48. "Dr. Criswell Charges Misrepresentation," *Dallas Morning News*, June 6, 1968.
49. Criswell, "Church of the Open Door."

pastors and theologians who fervently argue that the denomination is built on the very words of God as derived thorough exposition and expressed through expository preaching.

Ironically Criswell's racist past had overshadowed him and so in considering the nomination in his sermon, he stated that the SBC's leaders said to him, "Pastor, the presidency of the convention does not enter into this one way or another. Sometime, somewhere, this has to be faced, and now is the time to do it. We're going to do it now."[50] Criswell stated that the purpose of his sermon was to express his reason for suddenly changing his stance to welcome black congregants into his church and accepting the nomination. However, Criswell did not use biblical text. Instead, he used a narrative approach for his justification of abandoning his racist views to accept the nomination. Criswell said the following in that sermon:

> And finally, as I spoke to my brethren and compeers in the church, our deacons, I said, "And I bare my personal soul to you. I cannot describe how I have come to feel the weight of it and the burden of it. I cannot describe to you how I feel when I preach the gospel of the Son of God and call men to faith and to repentance, and then stand there afraid that somebody might respond who has a different pigment from mine. It is though I were living a denial of the faith, to preach and be afraid that somebody might respond."[51]

Criswell spoke about visiting children's homes, hospitals, and local colleges and seeing African Americans who were welcomed. He concluded the church should be equaling welcoming, and it was not until the end of the sermon that Criswell actually quoted several Bible verses, which were not a part of the text. Criswell utilized a technique disavowed by SB expositors and theologians known as proof-texting in which he identified specific text or a single verse to support his point without doing any details or paragraph analysis.

Proof-texting is the method by which specific sentences or verses are identified, isolated, and used without any references to their immediate context. This task is to identify a verse in the Bible and say this verse means something related to the topic at hand without examining the verse's location in the canon. For example, Matthew 23:9 states, "Call no man your father on earth, for you have one Father, who is in heaven." Proof-texting means this text can be used to denounce the Catholic tradition of bestowing

---

50. Criswell, "Church of the Open Door."
51. Criswell, "Church of the Open Door."

the pastoral title of Father or to denigrate referring to one's biological father as Dad.

In the SB expository approach, the pastor examines the paragraph in which the Matthew 23:9 passage appears and its role in the canon. This exegetical approach would reveal that Jesus, the true king of the Jews, is arguing with the Pharisees who were culturally seeking the honor of being proudly titled Father or Rabbi as described by Blomberg:

> Jesus now shifts from speaking about "them" to "you"—all those among the crowds and disciples (v. 1) who might still truly be or become his followers. He picks up on his observation about greetings from vv. 5–7 and warns specifically against imitating the Jewish leaders in this respect. The three titles he uses as examples of what to avoid are "Rabbi" (v. 8), "father" (v. 9), and "teacher" (v. 10). All commonly referred in Judaism to those who expounded the law. "Rabbi" etymologically meant *my great one*. "Father" was apparently reserved for the patriarchs and revered teachers from the past (cf. the allegedly oldest portion of Mishnaic tradition—the *Pirqe Aboth* or "Sayings of the Fathers"). "Teacher" (*kathēgētēs*) referred especially to a *tutor*. As with many of Jesus' teachings in the Sermon on the Mount, texts elsewhere in the New Testament make it clear that he is not promulgating absolute commands. People are properly called teachers in Acts 13:1; 1 Tim 2:7; and Heb 5:12. Paul will even refer to a spiritual gift that enables some people to be so identified (Eph 4:11; 1 Cor 12:28–29; cf. Jas 3:1). It remains appropriate to call a biological parent one's father, and even one's spiritual parent may be addressed with this term (1 Cor 4:15; cf. also 1 John 2:13; Acts 22:1). So the point of vv. 8–12 must be that such titles are not to be used to confer privilege or status.[52]

Blomberg used this approach to engage in a historical, grammatical, and linguistic analysis to understand the meaning of the verse and to connect the single verse in Matthew with its surrounding verses and the overall book of Matthew.

Surprisingly Criswell had made a pivotal decision without utilizing his own methodology. At stake were Criswell's ethics and morality. Unlike Patterson who was fired from his post as President of Southwestern Baptist Theological Seminary and lost several speaking and teaching opportunities, Criswell continued to rise and lead the resurgence of the convention. It is ironic in that Patterson helped spearhead aspects of the conservative resurgence. Both men demonstrated a lack of ethics and a sense of hypocrisy

---

52. Blomberg, *Matthew*, 342–43.

by acting without utilizing the methodology which they avowed the safest biblical method for making doctrinal stances. Patterson violated doctrinal stances when he did not follow basic doctrinal ethics, calling into question expository methodology as the true basis for SB communal doctrinal and dogmatic ideological stances. The concern regards whether or not the SBC is built on values that do not necessarily emanate from Scripture even though these values are socially accepted as conservative, given that conservative congregants comprise the majority of the SBC.

The SBC appears to propagate exegesis and exposition while being actually focused on supporting the conservative values that matter to its congregations and to their perceptions of being socially conscious community. Promotion of racial reconciliation could have been supported by expository methodology by Criswell; however, Criswell did not engage in exegetical analysis of any other passages. It does lead to another connected issue regarding how two biblical passages can contradict one another. Problematically, one produced an outcome based on expository methodology to support segregation and the other was accepted by the church and denomination in a positive light without being supported by exegesis and exposition.

Noteworthy is the ability to practice exegetical methodology and preach expositional sermons even when there is a lack of comprehensive biblical theology. The expositional sermon inaccurately represents the biblical stance on the subject matter without fully following exegetical methodology. In this case, one could argue that the Genesis 9 text was not a historical for the reason for segregation or racial inequality but a narrative account of primordial history. The text historically was not seeking to answer or address the issue of race as the genre analysis would show the text was a part of the recounting of Israel's history and God's dealings with mankind. A more appropriate posture by Criswell would have been to locate all the biblical text that dealt with the issue of racial equality to engage in an exegetical and expositional examination of the issue rather than focusing attention on one isolated verse of biblical text. It stands to reason that the SBC and its theologians and pastors must practice acritical, biblical voice in addressing contemporary issues and avoid doing so only when it is convenient for the advancement of the SBC's agenda, political goals, or communal appeasement.

One of Criswell's detractors, Stewart Neuman wrote accordingly to Criswell in a letter:

> It may be that you have not really changed, W. A. Perhaps you are giving yourself credit for having changed when what you are

now doing is what you have been doing very dramatically all the while—namely, telling the people what they want to hear.[53]

Conversely, Freeman suggested that Criswell had understood with greater clarity the political and social landscape of the 1980s "more clearly than anyone could have imagined. He was able to envision the passing of the Dixiecrat politics of the Solid South, and the emergence of a new conservatism that would fit like hand-in-glove with the New Religious Right."[54] Undoubtedly, Criswell's repudiation of Jim Crowism and racism contradicted the obstructionist views of many southern evangelicals but also did marshal a new tenure in SB polity. However, his lack of utilization of the expository methodology detracted from the renowned expository purism of SB theologians while carrying significant weight societally.

The SBC pastors and theologians as well as SB institutions of higher learning emphasize a commitment to biblical exegesis and expository preaching. Their expository stalwarts, such Criswell and Patterson and the SBC in general, have tended to deviate from the standard practice of biblical exposition. The SBC has utilized expository preaching to build and sustain the convention, and more specifically, local congregations. SBC pastors and theologians have contended that the innate quality of expository preaching makes it an accurate model and measure for preaching biblical truths to local congregations. This model ensures their message is accurate, credible, and believable. The doctrines and dogma that emanate from this methodology are expressions of divine ordinances that SB expositors believe will produce divine rewards and attract likeminded people to the SB community.

The SBC produces and attracts conservative minded adherents because of their commitment to conservative values. SBC pastors and theologians have built a community or communal aspect based on the dogmatic stances of the SBC. In some cases, they have adopted nonbiblical, yet conservative, values to appease their congregants. SBC pastors and theologians on occasion have violated their own biblical expository method when they have not supported clearly what are biblical causes or have ignored biblical injunctions. This observation calls into question their ethical or moral standards. One wonders if they are more committed to the communal aspect of the SBC and less so on the personal, individual characters found behind SB scenes. In other words, SBC pastors and theologians use the Bible to attract followers and sustain their numbers, but in critical or crucial scenarios, they also neglect to honor their foundational, expository methodology.

53. Letter from Stewart A. Newman to W. A. Criswell, July 18, 1968. Criswell's handwritten reply is written on Newman's letter, which he mailed back.

54. Freeman, "Never Had I Been So Blind," 12.

Chapter 4

The Translation Methodology of the SBC

IN CHAPTER 4, I focus on SBC translation methodology that supports the SB theologians's need for purity and literalness in understanding the Bible as written in the original Hebrew, Aramaic, and Greek. It is important to the SBC that the accuracy of the original biblical text is maintained. SBC pastors and theologians support a process whereby content is communicated in such a way that they maintain the exactness and naturalness of the original biblical text. The foremost SBC theologians and pastors envision themselves preaching from a book which embodied the very word of God. The Bible translation itself should be very close to and equivalent to the original autographs of the Scriptures. The Bible translation methodology is of great consequence to ensure the sermon is based on the original texts of Scripture. This is to ensure that the expository sermon can be said to reflect the originally intended meanings that were shared with the original audience.

The Veracity of the Literal Translation

SBC theologians need a Bible translation that maintains a literal rendering of the original. The translation should be literal in the sense that it is faithful to the original Hebrew, Aramaic, and Greek texts and uses a word-for-word instead of a thought-for-thought translation methodology. They validate their pulpit communication and assure congregants that their personal reading of the Bible is also a real rendering of the original text by having a close word-for-word translation at their fingertips. The retransmission of the exactness and literalness of the Scriptures is of paramount significance due to the foundational connection between text and sermon.

Additionally, there is a fundamental belief in the idea of the priesthood of every Christian adherent. This ideology serves as the backdrop of the Reformation and the basis of the translations of the books of the Bible into English. SBC theologians are concerned that their congregants have the written text of the Bible in the vernacular of the day. It is indispensable to the expository homiletic process that the preaching of the text is accompanied by the listener's personal reading and personal appropriation of the homiletic tenets addressed in the expository sermon. The translation of the Bible used to reference the expository sermon is of utmost importance. SBC theologians have maintained that the expositor should begin the hermeneutical process with an examination of the text in its original language. The sermon when communicated to the congregants should imitate or reflect the original language as much as possible to demonstrate the literalness and purity of the original biblical text.

The Bible translation used when delivering the expository sermon is of paramount importance, and until the 1950s, the predominant Bible translation used by SB expositors was the King James Version (KJV). It was the translation most people knew or to which people had access. This English translation of the Bible was studied, memorized, and oft quoted, and the language strongly influenced modern culture and society. SB preachers used the KJV to connect the sermon with the text, as they believed for a time, the KJV was the most accurate English language translation of the original language of the Bible. SBC theologians believed that the KJV preserved the intentions of the original biblical authors, and as such, transmitted the very words of God.

Michael Haykin, professor of church history and biblical spirituality at Southern Baptist Theological Seminary surmises that during the 1950s, the KJV was the version that most English-speaking Christians used. The KJV was the Bible used by most SB pastors as the Bible translation with which most adherents were conversant. The translators of the KJV had believed that their version would rouse morality and spirituality in societal cultures. "People like John Wesley and George Whitfield and Jonathan Edwards would all have used this version in their preaching. When the modern missionary movement begins with people like William Carey and Hudson Taylor and David Livingstone, this again is the Bible that's used through the 19th century," according to Haykin who added, "It's the Bible Charles Spurgeon would have preached from, and so on."[1] The SBC was committed

---

1. Roach, "Until the 1950s."

to the KJV because of the widespread popularity of this translation. It was the translation used in most SBC churches and in society. It was used to make references to texts in expository sermons, and it was the only Bible that most people knew. Admittedly, the KJV has maintained the greatest influence on modern culture over other Bible translations.

Even though SB expositors lauded the KJV, its language and style became outdated. In time, SB pastors and theologians began asserting that language changes and is never static. Hence, the move toward using other translations of the Bible by contemporary congregations began. The SBC supported translation projects such as the NKJV Bible translation. Nonetheless, the move to use a more contemporarily functional KJV translation was not published until the 1980s. The SBC strongly supported the effort by Bible publisher, Thomas Nelson Corporation, to modernize the KJV. Thomas Nelson undertook the translation project involving 102 scholars and linguists and produced an updated, but functionally equivalent NKJV.

SBC pastors and theologians utilized the NKJV because they had argued that the vocabulary, the idioms, and phraseology in the KJV are emblematic of the language and speech patterns of the Victorian era. Furthermore, they argued that the KJV sounded strange or foreign and lacked the clarity necessary to ensure that the congregants understood the literal meanings of biblical texts.[2] Because of the popularity of the NKJV, the Thomas Nelson Corporation published several NKJV translations as study Bibles that contain accompanying notes and commentaries such as *The Criswell Study Bible*.

SBC theologians asserted that the scriptural texts used by congregants should put the word of God in the language of the people. They pointed to the authors of the New Testament who wrote the original autographs in the common language of the people, and not in the Greek dialect of the academy (Attic).[3] SBC pastors and theologians have emphasized translations used by expositors and congregants should be in the common language of the congregants. The congregant should hear and read the literal translation of the text in the contemporary language of the day. The exposition should not only provide insight but also clarity regarding the literal translation of the scriptural text.

The SBC has for a long time used the experience of the Reformation to formulate their current position concerning their methodology of translating the Bible. SB pastors and theologians fear that the lack of accessibility to a literal rendering of a scriptural text in the language of the people or

---

2. Roach, "Until the 1950s."
3. Roach, "Until the 1950s."

the failure of pastors to preach from the Bible could lead to the problems caused the Reformation. They contend that the lack of access to scriptural text in the language of the people led to decadence and abuses by the Roman Catholic church. Haykin, notes that "a key thrust of the Reformation was to get the Bible to the people, which required translating it into the vernacular, the speech that people were using, instead of leaving the Bible in Latin."[4]

Also, there have been repeated calls for the use of translations, which only employ modern or contemporary language as a faithful or literal translation of the Bible. The contemporary SBC exegete is compelled to subscribe to a translation which maintains fidelity to the original so that the theological underpinnings of inerrancy and infallibility are the basis for the homiletic and sermonic presentation. The SBC expositor avoids certain translations because of his or her view of the nature of Scripture. SBC scholars argue for selecting a modern translation that can be used in public as well as private worship and study and to speak to the

> Common man who does not know the Lord. Choose a modern translation that follows these proven and venerable principles that have blessed the church for centuries. Choose a translation then (1) that translates faithfully and accurately the meaning of the original Hebrew and Greek without unnecessary interpretation, (2) that reflects a high view of Scripture, and (3) that—especially for our day—follows the natural changes of modern idiom, but does not follow unnatural language changes of political movements or agendas.[5]

Albert Mohler suggests that a good Bible translation involves the following:

> Taking the Word of God and translating it into the vernacular of a people who are deeply in need of the Scriptures and that it is a work that must be done with great skill and reverent care. He emphasized the importance of robust, sophisticated and literal translation of the Holy Scriptures.[6]

Aída Besançon Spencer argues for literal translations especially when studying about preaching or teaching. Spencer states that "a general exegetical rule is that when translating for interpretation, the more literal, the better; when translating for communication, the more dynamic and equivalent,

---

4. Roach, "Until the 1950s."
5. Fuller, "Choosing a Translation," 56–57.
6. Mohler, "Making."

the better."[7] In other words, for interpretation and preparation of expository sermons, form or language is more crucial.

The SBC has verbally supported and financially invested in literal or formal equivalent translations of the scriptural text beyond the NKJV. Once such translation published through Lifeway Resources, the publication arm of the SBC, is the Holman Christian Standard Bible (HCSB). In 2004, the SBC drafted the following resolution of support for the HCSB:

> To champion the absolute truth of the Bible against social or cultural agendas that would compromise its accuracy, LifeWay Christian Resources of the SBC has commissioned a new translation, the Holman Christian Standard Bible, that is faithful to the original languages and understandable to modern audiences.[8]

In contemporary times, SBC theologians and pastors have opted to use biblical text translations with literal renditions of the original languages contained in the Bible. SBC expositors are concerned that the translation is a faithful rendering of the original language. The more renowned pastors with larger congregations have opted to use literal Bible translations such as the NKJV, HCSB, or NASB. For instance, Second Baptist Church in Houston is the largest SBC church and currently uses the NASB. Greg Matte, denominational leader and pastor, uses the HCSB.

Dr. Charles Stanley, former president of the SBC, pastor of FBC Atlanta, and founder of In Touch Ministries, one of the largest radio and television broadcast ministries, recommends the HCSB for new converts and for scholars and theologians alike. Dr. Stanley believes that the HCSB translation is easy to read and thoroughly researched.[9] Denominational and influential national SBC leaders, such as Chuck Colson who founded the Prison Fellowship Ministries, have asserted that the HCSB translation is easy to read, contains a great reference system, and represents a faithful reproduction of the original texts. The translation team for the HCSB included the foremost SBC theologians and denominational leaders, such as David Allen, Thomas R. Schriener, George Klein, and Richard Melick, as its evangelical theologians and commentary writers. SB pastors relish utilizing a biblical translation derived from the literal renderings of the Bible's original languages so that their congregants can understand their divine messages easily. The HCSB represents a rendition for the expositor to use with assuredness regarding its faithfulness to the original languages in which the Bible's texts were written.

7. Spencer, "Exclusive Language," 392.
8. Southern Baptist Convention, "The Holman Christian Standard Bible."
9. Holman Bible Publishers, "Preface."

According to the SBC, the closer the connection and the more active the interleaving between texts, original languages, and sermons, the greater the probability that the congregants will hear an inerrant, infallible Scripture, and impactful expository sermon. The potency of the sermon is derived from an active reading and contact with the pure and literal Bible. The expository sermon explicates and transmits God's word in a palatable and edifying manner, but the Bible serves as the connection to and ongoing instrument of, or engine for, personal understanding based on the SB pastor's exposition of the text. For the exposition to be effective, the translation choice is one of paramount importance. SBC adherents use Bible translations including paraphrase versions to expose meaning in biblical verses, but they are devoted to using specific or particular translations for their expository sermon. Paraphrases or free translations are more likely to be used for comparative analysis, word studies, or colloquialization of seemingly archaic or wooden phrases.

SBC adherents use translations that are faithful and literal renderings of the original languages in which the biblical texts were written. SB pastors use the original languages in their preparation and hermeneutical study of the Bible and the literal translations to deliver their expository sermons. It is not simply a matter of methodology, but the epicenter of a Bible translation lies in its readability and tonal accuracy for correctly conveying the ideas of the sermon and the original text. That is why notable SBC preachers and theologians, such as Richard Jeffers, Ed Young, Matt Chandler, Mac Brunson, and Jack Graham, of some of largest churches in the SBC use literal biblical translations, such as the NASB or NKJV, as their main source texts for preaching. Foremost theologians Al Mohler, Paige Patterson, Daniel Akin, and David Allen use formal or literal translations as their source texts when delivering expository sermons. For Mohler:

> Every word of Scripture is inspired, [and] translators should aim for a formal equivalent translation . . . If we believe in a verbal doctrine of inspiration, then how can we believe in anything less than a verbal concept of translation? If we really believe in verbal plenary inspiration, then the words are important.[10]

Since verbal inspiration means that the original words of Scripture convey the ideas and thoughts that God intended, then Mohler is arguing that the expositor should use a translation that best expresses the literal or original words of the scriptural text to ensure that the expositor maintains the accuracy of the original. Mohler's point is that a literal translation of

10. Foust, "Mohler."

the Bible correctly interprets the original words of the scriptural texts, and that they are the best words to express the thoughts or ideas of the original. An examination of congregational use of the Scriptures over the past five years reveal that the dominant translations used nationally have been literal or formal translations. Notable is SB expositor use of the following literal, formal translations: KJV, NASB, New Revised Standard Bible (NRSB), and English Standard Version (ESV).

SBC theologians and pastors seek to ensure that the texts that they reference yield a literal rendering, due to their theological concern with inerrancy and verbal plenary inspiration. The choice of a translation is not necessarily dependent on providing congregants with easy biblical understandability but instead is on preserving the accuracy or the exactness of the original texts within the Bible. The SB expositor's commitment to formal equivalence is somewhat ironic because one of the goals of expository preaching is to bring clarity when conveying actual meaning. Formal equivalence translations do not always achieve that purpose as dynamic equivalent translations appear easier to read and understand and centers on faithfulness to the original language. Formal equivalence versions are translated word-for-word from the Greek and Hebrew texts to maintain grammatical structure and original language patterns as they can be replicated within a comprehensible English language presentation. The form and content of the original texts are reproduced for offering a faithful rendering of the original within the English language. A formal equivalence translation attempts to find as close a match as possible between English and the source language. Additionally, the goal is to ensure that the English-reading Christian can connect with the original context and situation of the source language and in some sense understand the culture, customs, and expression connected with the original setting.

A formal or literal English translation is designed to maintain as much of the source-language form and structure as possible. Accordingly, SBC expositors seek to situate the reader of the English in the *sitz-im leben*, or the cultural setting, of the source language to experience the culture and customs of the original audience. SBC expositors believe that when their congregants hear and experience the original wording and context, the congregants will be personally impacted and transformed in both behavior and mindset. Then, SBC congregants will believe and behave in accordance to the instructions that the expositor delivers and demands in his sermon.

Criticism of Dynamic-Functional Equivalence Translations

SB expositors believe that literal or formal translations enable the reader to connect and better comprehend the syntactic and semantic structures of the source language. Furthermore, the literal translation contains significantly less deviation from the source language form and structures in other translations. SBC theologians and pastors tend to avoid dynamic-functional equivalence translations as the main reference point for their sermons but use such translations to aid in their explanations of biblical concepts or ideas but not for expositing the main text of the sermon. Additionally, SB expositors prefer to show the congregation as close a match as possible to the original language's text and to use a literal translation Bible version when delivering expository sermons. However, when a concept needs a special or clear explanation, SB expositors reference a translation that presents the concept faithfully with contemporary language or jargon, and most often this is a dynamic equivalent translation.

SBC expositors and pastors focus on verbal plenary inspiration and exegetical hermeneutics so that actual words, sentence order, form, and structure maintain special importance. In their expository sermons, these issues become the highlights, or the mainstays, for conveying important theological thoughts and ideas. In other words, SB doctrinal ideology is built or founded on the systematic and canonical study or words, phrases, syntax of sentences, and the semantic domain of words. SB expositors show its occurrence in the receptor language and do word for word explanations as well as syntactical and semantic explanations. SBC pastors do see this process as adding to their credibility and authority to afford credence to the expository sermon as sourced from the original text, because the SBC places responsibility for to explaining scriptural text primarily on its pastors. SBC pastors and theologians are committed to the expository methodology as they believe it enables them to explain the text accurately and clearly.

Both SBC congregants and pastoral leaders focus on reading and referencing texts that edify original's rendering accurately. Their deference toward literal or formal translations was due in part to the fact that formal translations supported the doctrinal ideology of inerrancy and the tenets of canonicity. Literal translations reflect the SBC's ideological commitments in its publications and SBC entities. The SBC asserts that the literal translation finds its basis in the biblical text itself, and that the biblical evidence indicates that the biblical methodology of preaching involved explaining the original texts of Scripture and referencing the same original text. The SBC approaches Bible translation with a similar mindset that was mentioned in the biblical text of Nehemiah. When the exiles returned to the community, there was the need for translation. The priests and scribes read from the original and explained it to the congregants.[11] The SBC utilizes this same methodology and a majority of SBC pastors provide expository sermons using literal or formal texts and translate or give sense and meaning to the original text and literal translation. Translations that are not literal renderings do not accord the same level of veneration. SB expositors believe that non-literal translations do not embody the original texts's languages and are man-made, subjective accounts of the original biblical text. SBC pastors and theologians see these nonliteral, or functional, translations as full of potential for mistranslations of the scriptural text. Therefore, any use of reference to the dynamic-functional translation is limited or fully avoided.

The exception is the initial version of the NIV, though a dynamic or functional translation it is considered reliable. The SBC had participated in the development and publication of this dynamic or free translation so its acceptance and usage by SBC congregations was not overtly controversial. The SBC fielded its own scholars who contributed to the translation project. Furthermore, the translation committee required all members to sign a statement affirming the inerrancy of Scripture. The Committee for Bible Translation (CBT) chose teams of scholars (in all over one hundred theologians) to do the actual translation work. Notwithstanding, its conservative ecumenical acceptance, there were some dissenters to the use of the NIV. The critical issue was that this model of translation and the dynamic equivalence philosophy conflicted at times with the doctrine of verbal-plenary inspiration. If the original words of Bible result from divine transmission, then any amendment or variation not only demeans the integrity of the text but also reduces the efficacy of its exposition due to a functional equivalent translation. Furthermore, detractors assert that any translation emendation could distort the sense of meaning and degrade the authority of the Bible.

Expository preachers are mindful about the lack of a perfect one to one correspondence, and hermeneutically, there will always be some degree of interpretation. They assert that formal equivalency translations require a significantly lower degree of interpretative distortion by translators. The only major problem or concern that they identify with formal equivalence involves its lack of readability even as it is considered more accurate. However, the nondenominational, expository preacher John MacArthur, who is one of the leading expository preachers in modern times, claimed that "by its very nature, a translation based on dynamic equivalency requires a high degree of interpretation."

---

11. Neh 1:1–8.

SB theologians acknowledge that dynamic equivalent translations and paraphrased Bible versions are more readable, even though these translations focus on conveying an idea-for-idea rendering of the original. SBC expositors will not preach from a translation based on an interpretive methodology, because this type of translation focuses on communicating ideas or thoughts rather than the original words of the texts. SBC theologians assert that dynamic equivalent translations attempt to choose contemporary language convey the meaning of the original in a desire to be relevant and contemporary. These translation choices may stray from the exact intent of the original due to that desire for contemporary appeal.

The translators of the NIV Bible argue that language has changed significantly, specifically that the term man as used in the past iterations of dynamic communicating was a gender-inclusive term. The translators of the NIV assert that they seek only to produce updates to the text so that the Bible can be readable. They recognize that the heart of the debate is angst on the part of conservative theologians who seek to maintain theological dogma and eliminate the influence of liberal ideologies, such as feminism.[12]

NIV translators firmly believe that their methodology is not an attempt to influence or change any sort of theology but instead to reach the masses. The NIV translation committee has outlined the basis of its methodology and claimed that the version's changes and updates are warranted based on their research of language. They claimed that the changes or updates are needed for current culture to fit the framework of the expositors interested in making or presenting an accurate understanding of the text to contemporary readers because the main goal of expositors is the take the original and present it to congregants in an applicable and understandable manner. Furthermore, expositors have long supported translators who accurately reflect changes in the receptor's language though more formal or literal equivalence. The NIV committee attempted to explain the scope of their methodology as linguistically and theologically oriented.[13]

The CBT for the NIV was set on affirming their theological aversion to liberal ideologies. They affirmed their commitment to ensuring their faithfulness of the original text and ensuring God's and the Trinity's maleness are maintained. Members of the CBT did sign the Colorado Springs Guidelines (CSG), which was a document produced by a group of conservative evangelicals that included members of the SBC, who ardently believed in the Bible's inerrancy and verbal plenary inspiration. By signing the CSG, the CBT members demonstrated their commitment to conservative ideologies. The

---

12. NIV Translators, "Is the NIV Gender Neutral?"
13. NIV Translators, "Is the NIV Gender Neutral?"

CBT has consistently maintained that their updates and changes evolved as outcomes based on their linguistically and theologically oriented methodology. They contend that they never intended to distort any theology or methodology.[14]

The CBT argued for their concerns about the making the text readable and understandable and providing a means for the next generation to be able to apply the biblical text. It is noteworthy that the CBT affirms the SBC dogma of inspiration and inerrancy and bases their updates and changes on reaching members of current culture, something to which expositors adhere. Their goals, the CBT claims, are not merely linguistic, and certainly not ideological, but are a methodology immersed in producing a faithful, contemporary, and readable Bible translation.

The Use of Dynamic-Functional Translations in Expository Preaching

The concept of the functional equivalence model is not an altogether flawed or discounted translation model as seen in the mainstream acceptance of the NIV. This model according to Eugene Nida involves a three step translation process. Nida outlines a process whereby he reduces the source text to its most simple structure and form a well as locating the simple semantic meaning of the words. Nida suggested making the transference of meaning to the receptor language using the simplest structure and then locating a stylistically and semantically equivalent expression in the receptor language.[15] There is a belief that dynamic translation is a better representation of the task of translation or hermeneutics by forcing the translator to analyze the text in its original language to seek the best sense of thought or idea in the receptor language. Dynamic translation can maintain a level of integrity by finding a contemporary and easily understandable equivalent translation.

There are some SBC theologians who maintain that the task of interpretation serves the purpose of attempting to understand the meaning of the original text. Through the practice of homiletics, the interpreter attempts to present a contemporary understanding of the original. SBC theologians warn that translators of dynamic equivalence versions, such as the NIV, made translation choices and completed the transference without ensuring fit with certain doctrinal ideologies. Therefore, expositors point to moments in dynamic equivalent translations where the expositors rework or reword the translation to provide theological and doctrine clarity.

14. Committee on Bible Translation, *Preface of the New International Version*.
15. Nida, *Toward a Science of Translating*, 68.

Even in cases of dynamic equivalence translations bringing about clarity and readability, expository preaching advocates warn that the foreignness or ambiguity should be seen in the receptor languages for which literal translations tend to allow. This transparency helps the as the expositor explain the ranges of meanings to identify the correct interpretation of the text. Thus, both expositor and congregant see the ranges of meanings but also understand the correct meaning of the biblical text. For the SBC, expository preaching demonstrates the text's complexity but reveals the accurate meaning of the text and involves the congregant in the process of translation. Further, the congregant is brought into the process or task of translation for their understanding.

SBC adherents argue that this process builds doctrinal purity and demonstrates to congregants the source of their theological ideology while affirming its translation as coming directly from the original text's meaning. It is possible to engage in the task of translation, identify ambiguities, show the interpretive options, and discuss the ambiguities when preaching from a dynamic equivalence translation. The expositor could mention the interpretative options and emphasize his choice for his literal interpretation. This does take away from the process of expository preaching for the translation and hermeneutic aspects serve the purpose of determining the original meaning so that it can be presented homiletically.

Nonetheless, there is value in allowing the reader to experience ambiguities in the text. For instance, the popular text of Ps 23, de Waard and Nida objected to formal-equivalence renderings of Ps 23:1 which states, "The Lord is my shepherd, I shall not want." De Waard and Nida argued that changes to language use over time means that "*want* no longer means 'to lack' but rather 'to desire.'"[16] De Waard and Nida made a translation or interpretative choice based on a cultural or personal understanding of the original text. Theologians and expositors have long asserted the intransitive verb of want seen in Ps 23:1 means "to lack" or "to have a need," and Thomas has explained that Webster's New Collegiate Dictionary gives 'to be needy or destitute' as the first meaning of want and 'to have or feel need' as the second meaning of want. The idea of desire as a definition for want does not appear until the fourth definition of want. Thomas argued that *Webster's Third New International Dictionary* defines want as "to be in need" which is exactly what the psalmist intended to say.[17]

SBC scholars have argued that this is a case where a dynamic equivalent translation is not needed because the word is not ambiguous and that

---

16. Waard and Nida, *One Language to Another*, 9.
17. Thomas, "Principle of Single Meaning," 157.

dynamic equivalent translations sometimes make unnecessary changes in an effort to connect with contemporary culture. Also, the changes suggested by Nida are too far removed from the original idea that was verbally inspired. SBC expositors and theologians want their congregants to be exposed to the various levels of meanings and to personally experience the translation choices instead of being given an interpretative option that is based on a specific cultural vernacular. Even if congregants are not given the ranges of meanings, the expositors want them to acquire the correct meaning the first time or see the connection between their literal translation and the explanation in the expository sermon. The SBC theologians and expositors then are reluctant to use dynamic translations as the main reference point for their expository sermons because of the fear that they may contradict their doctrinal ideologies.

The SBC and the Production of Dogmatically Appropriate, Literal Translations

SBC has always been concerned that Bible publishers and translators engage in translation techniques that do not produce Bible versions that contradict SBC doctrinal ideologies. SB theologians and pastors remain wary of translations that contain gender-inclusive language, remove patriarchal references, or remove or reword references to sin for specific behaviors, such as homosexuality, gambling, drunkenness, partying or carousing, abortion, or inerrancy. The SBC does not approve of Bible translations that deviate from literal translations because doctrinal ideologies are sacrificed in the effort to connect to produce a contemporary translation. For the SBC, the sacrifice is too great.

The SBC recognizes that Bible publishers and translators want to produce a popular, contemporarily updated translation of the Bible, but these translation choices that would be embraced by culture contradict or soften traditional SBC doctrinal ideologies. Dynamic equivalence translations such as the updated 2011 version of the NIV, the Today's New International Version (TNIV), and the New International Version Inclusive (NIVI) Bibles were developed with translation principles allowing for gender-inclusive language as well as the removal or addition of references that conflict with or contradict traditional SBC ideologies. SBC pastors and theologians reject these translations as reaffirming cultural expectations and capitulating to the social norms of the day.

SBC leaders have worked to ensure that convention-approved Bibles include literal translations and that no Bibles contain dynamic translation choices and content contradictory to SBC historic or traditional theology. SBC leaders believe that literal translations must use word-for-word references to transfer the exact meanings, which they have used to establish their doctrinal foundation, from original languages. The SBC is aware of cultural changes leading to the acceptance of transgender and homosexual rights, causing ongoing abortion debates, and continuing feminist issues. The SBC has foresworn Bible publishers with translations failing to support SBC theological positions or choosing to include language that contradicts SBC doctrine. The fears of the SBC came to fruition with the announcement of the publication of the TNIV and its projected release in 2006. The TNIV was designed to reflect updates to the NIV translation.

The TNIV was also the work of the Committee on Bible Translation (CBT), a group of thirteen evangelical scholars who had also produced the translated NIV. However, in 2009 it was confirmed that publication would be discontinued and would be replaced by an updated NIV. The TNIV was to be based on the dynamic equivalence translation methodology and received widespread criticism, because it was to include gender-inclusive language that contradicted SBC doctrinal theologies. The translators of the TNIV wanted to produce an updated version of the NIV that would be readable and would reflect the current state of the culture. The TNIV would have contained limits to the use of language that would have indicated a male dominated society and would not have given preference to males over females. Also, the TNIV translation would have made God accessible to both male and female readers with the language of the Bible presenting God as caring or identifying equally with both males and females. However, these translation choices were what the SBC was apprehensive about when they formulated their resolution in 1997. They supported the production of the NIV but did not want to a translation that could change the literal meaning of the text, in this case, the details of meaning that are present in the original Greek or Hebrew text, especially details concerning Jesus Christ, to be published. The TNIV represented all the publication problems the SBC did not want to see, including gender-neutral language against which the denomination along with other likeminded theologians and scholars took a stand.

Douglas Moo was the chairman of the translation committee for the TNIV and sought to calm SBC leaders's fears by informing them that the TNIV was constructed on the principles of James Barr's *The Semantics of Biblical Language*. Moo contended the following:

> Linguistics is not a prescriptive but a descriptive enterprise; second, meaning resides not at the level of individual words but at the level of collocations of words in clauses, sentences, and

ultimately discourses; and third, the meaning of individual words is expressed not in a single word gloss but in a semantic field.[18]

Moo thereby suggested that a word for word substitution or the exactness of a particular phraseology is not necessary but that the theological point or idea of the text that was translated. The translation of the source language, for Moo, should be a theologically astute translation that preserves the intent of the original writer. Moo emphasized the need for theological correctness but focused on readability and relatability of the translation.[19] Moo's explanations about the TNIV did not lessen the angst experienced by the SBC. The SBC issued a resolution in 2002 denouncing the production, publication, sale, and translation methodology of the TNIV as follows:

> WHEREAS, Many Southern Baptist pastors and laypeople have trusted and used the New International Version (NIV) translation to the great benefit of the Kingdom; and
>
> WHEREAS, The International Bible Society (IBS) and Zondervan Publishing House have begun to publish a new translation of the Bible known as Today's New International Version (TNIV); and
>
> WHEREAS, Southern Baptists repeatedly have affirmed our commitment to the full inspiration and authority of Scripture (2 Timothy 3:15–16) and, in 1997, urged every Bible publisher and translation group to resist "gender-neutral" translation of Scripture.[20]

In the SBC resolution, the SBC declared that the TNIV contradicted the SBC doctrinal ideology of inspiration by containing language translated from the original text that had literally been clearly denoting the gender of male and using gender-inclusive language in the English translation. This translation technique did not follow the SBC doctrine of verbal plenary inspiration and opposed the theology of inerrancy and infallibility. The translation suggested the use of male dominated language was insufficient and incorrect, but the SBC argued that the translation undermined its view that the literal meaning or author's intended meaning was incorrect. The SBC believed that the translators of the TNIV were sacrificing theological or doctrinal correctness for readability. Furthermore, SBC leaders believed that the TNIV translators took liberties with the text by adding language that was not found in the original text and causing the Bible's text to be

18. Moo, "Bible and Translation."
19. Moo, "Bible and Translation."
20. SBC, "Resolution on Today's New International Version."

mistranslated. The SBC prohibited the sale of the TNIV in all of its stores and entities and disavowed its use in its churches or for private readings, which resulted in the early discontinuation of the TNIV.

The NIVI publication in London caused the SBC to become alarmed that translators would publish Bible versions that reflected societal or cultural changes that distorted SBC dogma. The NIVI was published by Hodder and Stoughton in London in 1996 and was only released in the United Kingdom. The SBC had hoped that the NIVI translators would have remained committed to inerrancy in producing dynamic equivalent translations that conveyed the sense of meaning or thought for thought but that would still not contradict SBC dogma or theological ideology. The SBC believed that the NIVI translation went against a commitment the translators affirmed with the production of the NIV. The SBC believed that NIVI's language included some intent to mislead congregants about the role of men and women and the nature of God. Its release in the United Kingdom mobilized the SBC and a host of like-minded social conservatives.

The NIVI alerted SBC theologians that the NIV translators may eventually engage in translation projects that would make changes to the Bible or updated the language to connect with contemporary culture. The NIVI suggested the future possibility of translators changing or removing biblical references to vices that literally render sin, such as homosexuality, transgender, gambling, drinking, or abortion. Focus on the Family's president James Dobson called in representatives of various church organizations, including SBC theologians and pastors, to oppose the NIVI and sign the thirteen CSGs or "Guidelines for Translation of Gender-Related Language in Scripture."[21] Dobson and SBC leaders were concerned that the NIVI overtly contradicted clear the biblical roles that had been operating within SBC churches for generations. Furthermore, the removal or reinterpretation of patriarchal terminologies detracted from the Bible's historical and cultural background. Also, expositors would have been challenged when writing sermons to reidentify biblical elements that had been deliberately obscured by NIVI translators.

If the NIVI had been released in the United States, it would have created a sense of theological angst and contradicted many of the pervading gender roles and patriarchal structures that exist in the SBC's ecclesiastic leadership. For example, SBC dogma would have been distorted and viewpoints or organizations that went against SBC dogma could have gained legitimacy within U.S. culture. The SBC viewed the NIVI translation as an attack on traditional SBC dogma, especially the notion of male leadership in

---

21 Grudem, "NIV Controversy," 3–6.

SBC churches, the idea of the maleness of Jesus, and the anthropomorphic male references to God in the Bible. The SBC did not see the NIVI simply as a mistranslation but instead as an intentional translation choice that called SBC dogma and values into question by removing male-dominated language from the Bible. SBC leaders believe that the NIVI translators intentionally sought to remove this notion of male-dominated leadership and to challenge SBC concepts of gender roles.

As a "people of the book," the SBC could not risk a Bible translation that contradicted SBC dogma. The Bible was the standard by which SBC congregants lived and operated. The support of a Bible version that contradicted SBC dogma by reputable translation committee could have resulted in a negative influence outside of the SBC on its congregants and the denomination as a whole. SBC leaders and pastors became focused on ensuring that formal equivalence translations were used in SBC churches and published by SBC entities. Also, the SBC actively discouraged the publication of any dynamic translation that contradicted SBC dogma and ideology, particularly that males are called to be leaders in the churches, homes, and society in general.

Historically, the SBC has held to the view of males having the access to SBC leader and pastoral roles in their churches, seminaries, and other entities as an inherently patriarchal viewpoint that the TNIV translation of the Bible contradicted. Therefore, the NIVI was an affront to the SBC's historical, biblical understanding of the Bible and its literal scriptural interpretations regarding biblical leadership. Additionally, the SBC saw the NIVI's gender-inclusive language for referring to God as a distortion of the original biblical texts's meanings. This translation shift was also received by the SBC as a direct attack on the integrity of scriptural text. Allowing gender-inclusive language to appear in an English translation of the Bible would have changed the SBC's foundational understanding of the Bible.

Clearly, any change of the original text is considered to have theological ramifications, such as the NIVI's use of gender-inclusive language to translate references to God. By using gender-neutral language, the NIVI indicated the presence of dual-natured or dichotomously-gendered God. Mass access to the NIVI translation could have created considerable problems for SBC theologians who argue ardently for a masculine Trinity due to the gender attached to Jesus and the Father that suggests the Holy Spirit is male. The SBC argument is that the original language should be translated literally, especially when referring to God.

Not only is the gender of God affected by the NIVI translation shifts but also the idea of original sin, the efficacious of salvation, the subordinate and functional role of women, and the leadership position of men are among dogmas affected in the presentation of this translation. The SBC believes in the functional or complementarian role of women. Women were created to help and follow the leadership of men. If women marry, they support their husbands's attempts to complete their divine purposes. The man is considered the leader and the woman must submit to his leadership in the church and in the home.

The translation choices for the SBC were not just theological but also ethical. SBC theologians and pastors see the NIVI as an ethical failure due to translators actively misleading congregants and readers of biblical text. This ethical misconstruction on the part of the translators of the NIVI was seen by the SBC as potentially undermining their entire denomination and calling into question certain SBC theological dogma. Moreover, SBC theologians would argue the inerrancy and infallibility of the original scriptural text was directly challenged by NIVI translators who made translation adjustments to reflect certain modern values. The SBC was particularly troubled by the IBS's team of Bible translators tasked with making the NIV and NIVI translations as well as with making future NIV publication updates and changes. The following five types of alterations account for over four fifths of all changes in the NIVI recommended by the IBS:[22]

a. From singular to inclusive plural (e.g. from "man" to "people"; 9 percent);
b. From singular to inclusive singular (e.g. from "man" to "person"; 15 percent);
c. From plural to inclusive plural (e.g. from "men" to "people"; 33 percent);
d. From indirect to direct reference (e.g. from "man's" to "your"; 9 percent);
e. From noun/personal pronoun to adjective/adverb (e.g. from "man's" to "human"; 15 percent).
f. Thirty references (or 12 percent of all changes made) involve a change in grammatical number (from singular to plural or vice versa.

The IBS expressed its unease with the CSG because the CSG document was produced by a group of conservative evangelicals, including SBC leaders, who ardently believed in inerrancy and verbal plenary inspiration. They provided specific guidelines for Bible translation in the wake of the proposed updates to the NIV and the publication of the NIVI. The IBS

---

22. Council for Biblical Manhood and Womanhood, "Neutering of 'Man' in the NIVI." Numerical breakdown is as follows:
  a: twenty-three changes
  b. thirty-eight changes
  c. eighty-three changes
  d. thirty-eight changes
  e. thirty changes

has difficulty with certain parts of the CSG, and "upon further review and consideration, and in consultation with other evangelical scholars, IBS has determined that many of the technical guidelines are too restrictive to facilitate the most accurate possible text in contemporary English."[23] The IBS's ongoing work has been conducted

> In accordance with its own guidelines, and the guidelines established by the International Forum of Bible Agencies," which encompasses "eighteen of the leading global translation ministries, including IBS, Wycliffe Bible Translators, United Bible Societies, Summer Institute of Linguistics (SIL), New Tribes Mission and others . . . responsible for more than 90 percent of the translation work done around the world [and seeking to do] uncompromisingly accurate translations in contemporary language.[24]

It is not surprising that the SBC had a clear preference for formal equivalence translations. Formal equivalence translations maintain distinct gender identification and patriarchal values. Formal equivalence translations avoid gender neutrality and convey the societal and cultural customs of the source language. Therefore, formal equivalence preserves the patriarchal structure of the Bible and allows for replicating patriarchal structures throughout contemporary conservative and mainline churches. Expositors can preach the text and use the translation to corroborate the elements of their homiletic treatises.

The SBC was concerned that gender-neutral translation would even affect the historical or traditional leadership framework of the church by distorting its principles on women in leadership. For example, while some SBC churches employ women pastors, the senior pastor or lead pastor is characteristically male. The SBC has articulated this structure in its position statement on women in ministry:

> Women participate equally with men in the priesthood of all believers. Their role is crucial, their wisdom, grace and commitment exemplary. Women are an integral part of our Southern Baptist boards, faculties, mission teams, writer pools, and professional staffs. We affirm and celebrate their Great Commission impact. While Scripture teaches that a woman's role is not identical to that of men in every respect, and that pastoral leadership is assigned to men, it also teaches that women are equal in value to men.[25]

23. Toalston, "Gender-Neutral."
24 Toalston, "Gender-Neutral."
25. SBC, "Position Statements: Women in Ministry."

SB churches may have male and female deacons; however, for the most part, the SBC theological position on women is they are complementarian to men who form church leadership. In the sense that women serve to help and support the leadership of men in SBC churches, their complementary role, even as they are considered equal in essence, requires women to serve a different function. Regardless, in the secondary structure, such as deacons, board of trustees, or committee leads, women play support role in the leadership structure. This is a tradition founded in the SB theological framework and is not considered to be based on any interpretative or subjective exposition. This tradition flows from a literal reading developed from a formal equivalence translation of the Scriptures.

The position of a major contemporary SBC congregation, the Village Church, is the following:

> While being absolutely equal in personhood and dignity, man and woman are distinct in their roles in the home and church. This position is to be distinguished from both ancient patriarchy that often neglects the equality of the sexes and egalitarianism which neglects the clear Scriptural role distinctions.[26]

Here, the Village Church asserted that men and women have distinct roles and functions, but the church attempted to show that the ancient biblical practices or beliefs that they believed to demean women, such as polygamy, women being only to work in the home, or women considered weaker in relation in men, were to be rejected.

While the Village Church sought to reject certain patriarchal beliefs it still maintained that the primary teaching or preaching role belonged to men and that final authority was the responsibility of the men in the church.[27] The core of the disagreement appears to have been concerned with the definition or meaning of "accurate." The SBC views "accuracy" as word-for-word transference that results in a literal rendering of the original text even though such translation can yield an archaic or wooden translation. The IBS translators argued for an accurate translation as one which resulted in the contemporary use of language but reflected the thoughts or ideas of the original biblical texts and authors. Therefore, for IBS, a translation would be considered accurate if it contained contemporary vernacular, maintained a semblance of the original meaning, and was easily readable.

Furthermore, the disagreement with the NIV translation committee about the NIVI, TNIV, and the gender-inclusive language updates to the

---

26. Village Church, "Complementarianism."
27. SBC, "Position Statements: Women in Ministry."

NIV represents a conflict between ideological positions. The SBC is concerned about the effect of liberal theology such as feminism and egalitarianism. The heart of the issue for the SBC is not necessarily the distinctiveness of language and the translation methodology employed by specific Bible translations but instead the perspectives that may lead to larger societal outcomes by reading the translation. Congregants could reject male representational leadership in their churches and homes. Congregants could embrace feminist values.

The SBC subscribes to a literal translation and finds significance in language constructs when using pronouns, proper nouns, and the gender under which nouns are subsumed. The tension point for the SBC is not necessarily about avoiding gender-neutral terms but is about the SBC view on the misuse of terms that clearly designate gender. The fulcrum of the argument for the SBC is that specific words and their gender designations have profound ramifications for SBC's theology of marriage, gay rights, civil liberties, feminism, and gender roles in general.

The IBS position about the NIV, even though the TNIV publication was discontinued and the NIVI was never published in the US, alarmed the very core of SBC expositors and theologians. In a sense the IBS was arguing that a majority of translators responsible for both formal and dynamic equivalence translations agreed that a gender-inclusive translation was necessary and theologically appropriate. James T. Draper Jr., then president of LifeWay Christian Resources of the SBC, stated that,

> LifeWay is committed to biblical accuracy, as seen in our new translation, The Holman Christian Standard Bible. While the International Bible Society has not specified the items from the Colorado Springs Guidelines it finds restrictive, our hope is that they will remain true to accepted evangelical scholarship. We have not seen their manuscript and will withhold judgment pending a review of the translation.[28]

The SBC wanted to ensure that IBS did produce a gender-inclusive translation which would oppose SBC dogma, but more importantly, the SBC believed that the move to a gender-inclusive translation ironically could not reflect the best work of biblical translation from an academic standpoint. The SBC sought to question the quality of scholarship or theological effort that would be utilized by the IBS. The SBC argued that the IBS translation represented an attempt to connect with culture by compromising the language of the original biblical texts. The SBC viewed the work of translation by the IBS as an ethical and theological misstep for purely aligning the

---

28. SBC, "Position Statements: Women in Ministry."

translation with what contemporary culture believed and wanted to see in the Bible.

The IBS translators on the other hand claimed to their goal was to produce a readable and understandable translation for contemporary readers. However, by so doing, the IBS translators incorporated words and concepts that were not in the original biblical texts. In a sense, they presented an "inaccurate" translation of the Bible. Nevertheless, the IBS translation strategy did not appear to be an intentional attempt to distort traditional SBC dogma. The IBS translators sought to produce a Bible translation that resonated with contemporary readers as a simple and easy to read and could be interpreted without the aid of an expositor.

SBC theologian and pastor, Albert Mohler explains:

> For no one who loves and respects the Bible would accept anything less than total accuracy as the goal of translation. The real issue here is a desire to update Bible translations to meet modern gender concerns. This is unavoidably ideological.[29]

Mohler is expressing concern that translators will make changes to appease certain groups over time, and such changes could lead to a different Bible altogether independent from the original biblical texts. Thus, the SBC believed that the scriptural text should maintain its inerrant and infallible form, because the NIVI and TNIV translations provide evidence that biblical text is susceptible to cultural pressures. Wayne Grudem comments on the TNIV which SB considered the basis for the 2011 updates by noting the egalitarian translation changes:

> In 1 Timothy 2:12 the TNIV adopts a highly suspect and novel translation that gives the egalitarian side everything they have wanted for years in a Bible translation. It reads, 'I do not permit a woman to teach or to assume authority over a man'. . . If churches adopt this translation, the debate over women's roles in the church will be over, because women pastors and elders can just say, "I'm not assuming authority on my own initiative; it was given to me by the other pastors and elders." Therefore, any woman could be a pastor or elder so long as she does not take it upon herself to "assume authority." So, it is no surprise that egalitarian churches are eager to adopt the TNIV.[30]

Grudem summarizes his examination of the gender-neutral changes and writes, "I am concerned that evangelical feminism (also known as

---

29. SBC, "Position Statements: Women in Ministry."
30. Grudem, *Evangelical Feminism*, 260.

"egalitarianism") has become a new path by which evangelicals are being drawn into theological liberalism." Grudem's argument is that the TNIV translation presents a view of women as equal to men in exercising authority in local churches and receiving the power to preach. Grudem asserts that the translation frees women to take the initiative to lead and teach with the caveat that they are not trying to usurp male leadership but that they are simply using their skills and God given abilities. However, Grudem does not observe a mere translation move to update the language by the TNIV and suggests that gender-neutrality is a liberal move on the part of the TNIV translators to cajole congregants to accept an ideology that is far too openminded for conservative theologies. Grudem assesses the translation updates and new translations as an attempt to take orthodox theology into the sphere of liberalism and to influence conservative denominations to take on liberal ideologies.

Ken Hemphill, theologian, denominational leader, and pastor expressed his concern that the IBS was instigating a theological change in response to a cultural change. The SBC is unyielding in its commitment to formal equivalence and reluctant to adjust to any changes impacting a literal translation. Hemphill promotes being careful always when,

> Taking the cultural climate of our day into consideration when retranslating Scripture because culture will change again. Our mission is not to make the Bible relevant to culture but to bring culture under the rubric of Scripture. It is the parameter under which we work.[31]

The SBC believes that the scriptural text should be fixed in meaning and translations must reflect the original biblical text. SBC theologians view the dynamic equivalence translations, such as the updated NIV, TNIV, NIVI, NLT and NCV, as attempts to produce a naturalness of expression and convey the culture of the original in manner that is understandable. However, the SBC notes these translations have changed the words, concepts, and cultural expressions to the extent that they contradict SBC ideologies and traditional dogma that are based on expositional preaching.

In some cases, the inclusion of certain vocabulary in the translations leads to a new or different understanding of the biblical text than what the original biblical text conveyed. Hence, the SBC views with suspicion the dynamic equivalence translation methodologies. The goal, as Hemphill mentioned, concerning the work of the translation and exposition is to express the original in the receptor language using a word-for-word

---

31. Grudem, *Evangelical Feminism*, 260

correspondence that conveys the original meaning so that congregation can understand and act on the original meaning, even if this meaning conflicts with contemporary culture.

Paige Patterson considers the IBS gender-neutral strategy to be an ethical and theological aberration. Patterson comments that imposing the gender-neutral ideology on the original text provided by John, Paul, Isaiah, Moses, and others changes the meaning of "what they wrote and often what they meant. It is fundamentally simply dishonest and grossly unfair to the writers of Scripture."[32] Patterson reports being "appalled but hardly surprised by IBS "pursuing its longstanding goal of a so-called "inclusive" language version of the Bible" because "if you issued a 'gender-neutral' version of Shakespeare, it would be the imposition of ideology on what the English bard believed and wrote."[33] Patterson explicitly refers to IBS as erroneously inserting or creating meaning in the original text that was never intended to be there by the Scripture's original writers. The heart of the matter for Patterson involved the IBS as imposing a new theological dogma on a translation destined for mass production worldwide that conflicted with SBC dogma. The IBS's translations, if embraced, would change traditional understanding of various theological dogma. The proposed updates and changes to the TNIV and NIVI would have led to structural changes in church leadership, understanding of gender roles, and even how sexuality is viewed. Any embrace of the TNIV or NIVI among congregants could have caused severe dissonance in local SBC churches.

The dynamic equivalence translations of the NIVI and TNIV are not trusted nor are expositions tied to those texts by SBC pastors and theologians. The SBC was very much concerned on theological as well as ethical grounds. The SBC expositor believes that it is his responsibility to fill in gaps when the literal rendering seems outdated or conflicts with current culture. SBC expositors believe that their role includes explaining the text and providing clarifications or extended expositional explanations when a clear one-to-one correspondence of the original language in the Bible translation is not evident. SBC expositors argue that when current language appears not to be sufficient or is inadequate for explaining the original text, it is the expositor fulfills the task of using homiletical techniques to help bridge any gap in understanding.

The NIVI could have had profound ramifications for the theological foundation of the SBC, and their clamor is not surprising. The changes included in the NIVI were not mere grammatical, cosmetic changes, but it

---

32. Grudem, *Evangelical Feminism*, 260
33. Grudem, *Evangelical Feminism*, 260

contained instances when Jesus's maleness was seemingly disregarded for a more palatable reading from as in the case of the John 10:33 translation from "mere man" to "mere human being." Jesus is foundational for the SBC and his male personhood is intricately connected to concept of substitutionary atonement through which the potency or efficaciousness of Jesus's sacrifice on behalf of human beings is derived. Through Old Testament theology, the male animal sacrifice hearkens to the sacrificial work of Jesus, a male God who covers the sin of the male Adam. Adam was the first man of all humanity who preceded the appearance women and children in God's creation. Jesus is considered the "second Adam" and represents the reversal of the man Adam's first failure.

The salvific work of Christ is the centerpiece of SBC theology. The nomenclature of "man" or "one man" postulates the unique work of the hypostatic union and not merely a generic human involvement in the affairs of humanity. Two versus are instructive as to the distinction between the literal and gender-neutral translations of the NIV and the NIVI. Of note, the critical words affected by the NIVI translation from the NIV translation are italicized to promote the reader's understanding of this analysis.

In the NIV, John 11:50 (NIV) is worded as: "You do not realize that it is better for you that *one man* die for the people than that the whole nation perish." In the NIVI, John 11:50 reads as: "You do not realize that it is better for you that *one person* die for the people than that the whole nation perish." When speaking about the resurrection of Jesus, in the NIV, 1 Cor 15:21 denotes: "For since death came through a *man*, the resurrection of the dead comes also through a *man*." However, in the NIVI, 1 Cor 15:21 reads: "For since death came through a *human being*, the resurrection of the dead comes also through a *human being*."

Historically, the SBC saw the proposed changes as a direct attack on the theological belief of Jesus as distinctly male and representative of the male sacrifice. In the Old Testament, male animals were sacrificed to atone for or pay for the wrongs or sins of men. Jesus represented the human male parallel to the male animal sacrifice, which is considered appropriately literal as a translation of original biblical text to the English biblical text.

SB theologians sought to address the concerns through not only the CSG but also through various theological studies and publications. The SBC worked alongside the Council for Biblical Womanhood and Manhood (CBMW). The partnership included several major SBC denominational leaders, pastors, and theologians, such as David Akin, Thomas White and Denny Burk serve on the Board of Directors, to produce several articles critical of the NIVI and TNIV and the proposed translation techniques used by the NIV translators.

The SBC and CBWM coalition argue that the NIV translators have neutered the Bible in by downplaying the masculinity of Jesus and that the unique teaching role assigned to men in Scripture has been diluted with the use of gender-inclusive language in places where previously the text referred to males teaching the pastoral letters and in the Scriptures in general. Furthermore, the SBC and CBWM argue that the gender of the Old Testament priests and prophets have been disregarded in the use of gender-inclusive language; they believe this change is an attempt to change how the Scriptures guide the roles of men in local churches.[34]

Paige Patterson has expressed feeling encouraged by the stance of the SBC and believes the SBC will continue to oppose gender-neutral translations for protecting their theological dogma. Douglass Moo, chairman of the translation committee, has responded to the concerns of the SBC. Moo makes the point that the updated translation presents the language of the Bible in a readable manner. Moo is not concerned with theological dogma but wants Bible readers to be able read a translation that reflects the current vocabulary of the receptor culture. Moo and the translation committee seem to be more concerned with contemporizing the language of the Bible rather than fulfilling any denomination's theological agenda. Moo sees in the translation process as a way to make gender-inclusive changes which are warranted based on contemporary English usage. Moo approaches the translation project simply from a functional position in which dynamic equivalence yields a simpler, easier reading or understanding of biblical concepts.[35]

In somewhat surprising move, the Trustees of LifeWay Christian Resources has voted to continue selling the new NIV Bible in LifeWay stores in a meeting of its Trustees that occurred on February 13 and 14 of 2012. The trustees had appointed a special task force to examine the nonbinding resolution approved by the 2011 SBC for requesting that LifeWay not sell the 2011 NIV Bible in its stores. Adam Greenway, committee chairman, commented that LifeWay's decision was made after "vast amounts of scholarly research and other relevant information was gathered and studied . . . and a number of subject matter experts [were] addressed the task force." Furthermore, Albert Mohler, president of Southern Baptist Theological Seminary; Russell Moore of Southern Seminary; Jimmy Draper, former president of LifeWay; George Guthrie of Union University; and Douglas Moo, chairman of the CBT that had translated the new NIV, supported LifeWay carrying the 2011 NIV Bible. Greenway, then told LifeWay trustees that "messengers

34. CBMW, "Neutering of 'Man.'"
35. CBMW, "Neutering of 'Man.'"

to the 2011 SBC annual meeting were encouraged to vote for the resolution based on incorrect information." Greenway added, "It is not that we are endorsing the 2011 NIV. We endorse what we publish, and the translation we publish is the Holman Christian Standard Bible. That is the translation that we endorse." Greenway also told trustees, "We do not believe the 2011 NIV rises to the level to where it should be pulled or censored or not carried in our retail chain."

The decision to change course by LifeWay is surprising because of the doctrinal concerns expressed earlier by SBC leaders and theologians. However, the NIV's connection with the SBC's marquee commentary series and its historical ties to Zondervan publishing made it almost untenable to pull the translation from its stores or seek to harm its sales when the NIV was so closely tied with LifeWay's own commentary series, and for that matter, several major commentary and technical Bible resources.[36] Of concern for SBC theologians and pastors, aside from the theological questions, were the associated changes toward a liberal viewpoint in the NIVI, TNIV and 2011 NIV. In other words, SBC theologians and pastors believed that the core tenet of the debate was over the symbolic value of the language within a larger cultural conflict, as opposed to the referential value of the words themselves. The SBC believed that these translations amounted to an attempt to liberalize the Bible and the SBC's congregants.

The NIV was very popular causing SBC theologians and pastors to expect the translation changes to be accepted and affirmed by popular culture and used to sway SBC congregants against following and supporting SBC ideology. The comments of Mohler indicate that the larger issue at stake is a concern about the move toward liberalizing the denomination.[37] Mohler is concerned about translations that do not have an ideological or political influence; hence, his urgent concern is that Bible translations reflect the conservative SBC ideology. The underlying issue is not simply the degree of language used and how that language reflects a formal or a dynamic equivalence methodology. The SBC seeks to ensure that Bible translations, and more so popular translations such as the NIV (which is has close connection with), maintain the conservative viewpoints of the SBC denomination. The sacred dogmas of the SBC are meant to be protected, and the SBC wants to ensure that other political or social perspectives enter SBC churches.

---

36. King, "LifeWay to Continue."
37. Toalston. "12 Evangelical Leaders."

Conclusion to Translation Methodology

The SBC is obdurate in protecting the ideological stance of male representation in its leadership and maintaining the corollaries of this doctrine. The linguistic concern about gender-inclusive language involves fear of allowing the egalitarian theology which leads to feminism and liberalism infiltrating congregants.[38] The overarching concern extends from a purely language-oriented debate to a fear of the acceptance and practice of so-called liberal theological ideologies. If the liberal theological ideologies gain acceptance and normative adherence among congregants through the very book that the SBC consider sacred for providing the guidelines for life, SBC doctrinal purity could be threatened. The SBC considers the Bible to be inherently authoritative. If the most popular translation with which it supported and partnered produced a translation containing contradictory ideology or potential theological dissonance, the threat to SBC doctrinal purity would lead to congregational dissonance, or worse, could lead to doctrinal revolution.

SBC adherents argue that the language of the Bible communicates both denotative and connotative aspects of each word, phraseology, and syntactic construction; additionally, are all of these imbued with a definitive theological substance. Specific words and gender form construction convey some sense of theological belief or foundational theological ideal. It is no surprise that arguments against gender-neutral translations do not center on the mere accuracy of the words but on the discriminatory demarcation of gender that is basic to SBC biblical traditional norms and values. The SBC attempts to convey or express its version of morality through its explication of the Scripture that corroborate its traditionalistic values. SBC theologians's and pastors's views of transgenderism, homosexuality, gay rights, and same-sex marriage are grounded on the nature of biblical words, names, and pronouns. The significance and concern with gender-neutral translations and versions of the Bible that untowardly neutralize biblical texts stem from this position. SBC constituents argue that gender in the Bible is the determining factor that has shaped the SBC's approach to social life and community life. The preaching in SBC churches has delineated an approach that will not allow for recognizing same-sex rights, transgender rights, or gender-neutral Bibles. The heart of the issue for SBC leaders and theologians is not the use of gender but the stipulation that gender denotes a particular perspective, namely a traditional biblical approach to interpreting and translating the Bible.

However, there is a need for biblical readability for understanding Scripture without alterations that amend the meaning of the original. The

---

38. Grudem, *Evangelical Feminism*, 260.

translation of the NIV and TNIV are not intentionally attempting to influence theology or challenge traditional SBC dogma. They too are pursing "accuracy" in the realm of relevance for contemporary readers. The translators desire for modern day readers to gain a sense of the original meaning in their own vernacular. The SBC believe that the NIV and NIVI translators have become too liberal with their use of dynamic equivalence updates that challenge historical, traditional SBC dogma as well as sacrifice or distort original biblical texts. One could say that the SBC's wooden or literal translations may not necessitate expository preaching but may also create a distance between the modern reader and scriptural text. This distance may result in a perception of the Bible as outdated and irrelevant. The conflict lies in dogmatic understanding and perception of the word "accuracy" and whether it is permissible or possible to translate readable biblical texts without challenging traditional SBC theological dogma.

Chapter 5

Social Impact on Culture

THIS FINAL CHAPTER CONTAINS the social and political views that emanate from SB theologians, pastors, and leaders engaging in expository preaching to influence political establishments through their theological stances. I will show that the expository method was a potent methodology for affecting social and political change and for galvanizing the polity for social, cultural, and political causes. In order to demonstrate their social and political influence, I report on opinion polls, newspaper articles, politicians affiliated with the SBC as well as their voting records and what laws they supported or enacted, effectiveness of funding of lobbying organizations, listenership and viewership of SBC radio and TV broadcasts, SBC churches's attendance records, and the convention's commercial enterprises and publications. I argue that the use of expository preaching has garnered widespread appeal due to its sacrosanct association with the objective truth divined from God's word. Therefore, the social issues supported by the SBC warrant a hermeneutical and homiletic model that supposedly maintains the veracity of their beliefs. I examine the works that have detailed the ideological and political conflicts in the SBC in an effort to show how their approach had an impact on the SBC and in national and social arenas. By examining the role of expository preaching and its espousal by the SBC in the twentieth-century, I will demonstrate the influence of the exegetical, hermeneutic, and translation methodologies in not only increasing or building a denomination but also affecting social and political change.

The Goals of Southern Baptist Pastors, Theologians, and Leaders

The SBC has asserted that its theological or biblical hermeneutical model determines its conservative social view. However, it is apparent that in some cases it is the social issues and views have shaped SBC social positions. These social views are propagated in SBC pulpits, seminaries, and literature. The SBC has sought to influence society and culture with its prevailing biblical views regarding cultural issues and ideas. Oftentimes the SBC biblical view clashes with the views of mainstream society and culture. However, the SB belief that expository preaching is based on true historical events as well as ancient, historical, and theological principles which transcend culture and time. SB theologians and pastors argue that their views are accurate and relevant for contemporary times. This SBC has sought to use the expository method to promote conservative social values and beliefs and to build community, or to be communal. The SBC has also used the expository methodology to frame responses to various social issues and events or to influence culture. In other words, their methodology serves not only the purpose of building community but also the purpose of influencing culture.

The goal of the SBC is not just to influence their local congregants but also to attempt to shape culture so that the society in general practices the biblical injunctions that they preach and teach in their local churches. Consequently, the SBC influences communities in the United States to adopt and practice SBC doctrine and dogma. The SBC inherently believes in itself as a steward of divine truth that should be followed by the general population. Furthermore, the SBC believes that when the text of Scripture is followed, there are individual benefits, and the more individuals obey the Scripture, the better it is for the population in general. Hence, society and culture would be better if they follow the expository teachings propagated by the SBC.

The SBC does its utmost to influence and control legislative decisions so that the laws and practices of culture do not conflict with or contradict SBC doctrine and dogma. Hence, the SBC is actively involved in politics and society for not only building community but also attempting to ensure that society is preserved from degradation. The SBC seeks to use the enactment of laws to support the practice of principles that fit SBC dogma. The SBC actively advocates and lobbies governmental leaders not for gaining converts but for building a society to reflect their ideals.

The SBC believes that the practice of expository preaching is the most accurate and historically true methodology for preaching and communicating the biblical text and so principles which are beneficial for the individual, church or the nation of Israel can also be helpful or useful for any individual notwithstanding their theological persuasion. Therefore, the interpretation of any biblical text by SBC preachers and teachers is accurate in demonstrating theological concepts for daily living for everyone.

Moreover, the SBC believes that the translations they use and recommend reflect their conservative interpretation of the biblical text, so that parishioners are not only privy to the original text during the preaching moment but also have a personal translation which reflects a faithful representation of the original. In short, the SBC's commitment to expository preaching then is based on the historicity of biblical text and the exegetical and translation methodology associated with expository preaching.

These tenets form the foundation for its approach to the Bible and serve as the mode for understanding and delineating their views of social and political issues in the United States of America. They also serve as the basis by which they defend their conservative social and political stances. The SBC believes in its divine responsibility to enforce its beliefs about the Bible in all churches and to ensure that no laws encroach on the SBC's right and freedom to practice its biblical beliefs. Furthermore, the SBC has forcefully argued against any governmental law that contradicts with its biblical view of culture and society. Whenever there is an issue that clashes with SBC views of what should be practiced in local communities, within states, and nationally, the SBC lobbied, protested, as well as galvanized its parishioners to counter these perceived social infractions.

SB leaders in order to protect their tax-free status and to give the appearance of being autonomous utilize specific agencies or organizations to influence political leaders such Family Research Council (to fight abortion), Lifeway Resources (media publications to support SBC values), North American Mission Board (to help specific countries or areas), Ethics and Religious Liberty Commission (separation of church and state and personal and church rights). Albeit there have been times when foremost SBC church leaders have come out openly and supported political candidates and the Republican Party.[1] The most shocking continues to be Dr. Robert Jeffress's support of then-Republican candidate for President Donald Trump and his various economic and social policies. Jeffress is the pastor of FBC Dallas and he has campaigned for Trump, supported his immigration policies, and his foreign policy strategy for North Korea, the building of the border wall, Trumps disdain for athletes that kneel during the anthem etc.[2]

Needless to say, their commitment to expository preaching has resulted in the SBC perpetuating certain theological stances that have a profound

---

1. Luigo, "Lobbying for the Faithful," 1.
2. Young, "Guide to Robert Jeffress," 1–2.

impact on twenty-first American culture. The SBC does not shy away from controversy but instead seemingly confronts cultural or societal practices and utilizes the biblical texts to attack the SBC's perceived problem. The SBC has been steadfast in supporting certain biblical positions because they believe it is based on the accurate and truthful rendition of the original text. Notwithstanding, there are several foundational stances to which the SBC adheres which exist against prevailing cultural and social norms. For example, SBC conservative social values include, alcohol abstinence, anti-gambling, pro-prayer and faith-based curriculums in public schools. However, the social values the SB believe warrants their proclamation and exposure and ardent support are the focus of this conclusion chapter.

First, the SBC's positions regarding marriage as between a man and woman, divorce as anti-biblical, and same-sex marriage as a sin are explicated. Additional focus is given to the SBC's pro-life and anti-abortion advocacy, pro-Israeli support, influence on the government and economy. The SBC as a biblical witness influence contemporary culture through the media completes the discourse. This final chapter ends the study with a conclusion to the SBC expository of homiletic theory.

Marriage, Divorce, and Homosexuality

For instance, in 2015 the pending judicial decision over gay marriage resulted in severe angst amongst the SBC. Ronnie Floyd and elected leader of the SBC at that time avowed "the Supreme court of the United States is not the final authority nor is the culture itself. The Bible is God's final authority on marriage and on this book we stand."[3] Floyd's comments were met with an overwhelming series of applause and ovations from thousands of SB messengers meeting in Columbus, Ohio.

In Texas, FBC Dallas, long considered the most conservative megachurch in the SBC, has consistently derided the efforts of the gay community to seek equality with certain civic rights. Furthermore, FBC Dallas church has demonstrated strong stances against the Supreme Court's decision to legalize same-sex marriage and was overtly critical of the Obama's administration attempts to redefine traditional and cultural understanding of the Bible. Dr. Robert Jeffress, pastor of the historic FBC Dallas, lamented in his expository sermon about issue of same sex marriage. Jeffress stated that the Supreme Court decision was an "affront in the face of Almighty God" as

---

3. Toalston, "Floyd and Former SBC Presidents."

well as the "greatest most historic landmark blunder in the history of the United States Supreme Court."[4]

Ironically, Jeffress's statements are indicative of the SBC's failure to deal with issue of slavery utilizing their own expository theological method. Jeffress also said that same-sex marriage is a "degradation, depravity and sexual perversion" and lambasted the Obama administration's decision to light up the White House in rainbow colors to commemorate the Supreme Court's decision.[5] Jeffress and his congregation remain adamant that the legalization of the same-sex marriage is a clear violation of biblical teaching and is prohibited in Scriptures. Jeffress's exposition of Scriptures led to his disparagement of same-sex marriage in a sermon entitled "The New Moral (Dis)order" in which he explained that God created two distinct genders with clarity of difference in both constitution and function. Jeffress alluded to the scriptural injunction against homosexuality in both the Old and New Testament and the Bible's prohibition against homosexual marriage.[6]

Specific texts which deal with the issue of homosexuality describe homosexual behavior as a person who is attracted sexually to members of his or her own sex. Lev 20:13 states that its practice warranted divine judgment, and Sodom and Gomorrah (circa Gen 19:4–5, 12–13) were destroyed because of the prevalence of homosexuality in these cities. The apostle Paul listed homosexuals among "the unrighteous" who would not inherit the kingdom of God (1 Cor 6:9), and stated that God's wrath stands against such behavior, whether practiced by men or women (Rom 1:26–27).[7] A SBC exposition of the text which address homosexuality in detail is the passage in Romans and appears in an SBC publication:

> Although God is "immortal" (*aphtharton*), humans are only "mortal" (*phtharton*). To exchange the one who exists outside of creation, not subject to its inevitable demise, for that which at the very moment is caught in the process of decay indicates the abysmal ignorance of fallen humans. In Deut 4:16–18 God prohibited the Israelites from making images shaped like a man, any animal on earth, or any creature that moved along the ground. Paul used these same categories to describe the flight of sinners away from the knowledge of God. This decline from idols shaped like humans, to images of beasts, and even to creeping things shows that a debased mind gravitates to the lowest possible level.

4. Jeffress, "New Moral (Dis)order."
5. Jeffress, "New Moral (Dis)order."
6. Jeffress, "New Moral (Dis)order."
7. Youngblood, *Nelson's New Illustrated Bible Dictionary*.

People cannot turn their backs on God with impunity. They exchanged the majesty of God for images made by their own hands, so God "gave them over . . . to sexual impurity." The verb has a certain judicial quality. The NIVSB note on 1:24 says, "God allowed sin to run its course as an act of judgment." God's wrath mentioned in Romans 1 is not an active outpouring of divine displeasure but the removal of restraint that allows sinners to reap the just fruits of their rebellion. F. Godet writes that God "ceased to hold the boat as it was dragged by the current of the river." The TCNT says that God has "abandoned them to impurity." Moral degradation is a consequence of God's wrath, not the reason for it. Sin inevitably creates its own penalty. "One is punished by the very things by which he sins" (Wis 11:16). Through the psalmist God declared, "My people would not listen to me . . . so I gave them over to their stubborn hearts to follow their own desires" (Ps 81:11-12). Divine judgment is God permitting people to go their own way.[8]

A non-SBC exposition but employing a similar methodology reveals:

In the Greco-Roman world homosexuality was quite common and even highly regarded, as is evident from Plato's *Symposium* and Plutarch's *Lycurgus*. It was a feature of social life, indulged in not least by the Gods (e.g., Zeus' attraction to Ganymede) and emperors (e.g., Nero's seduction of free-born boys was soon to become notorious). The homosexual reputations of the women of Lesbos was well established long before Lucian made it the theme of his fifth *Dialogue of the Courtesans* (second century a.d.). But Jewish reaction to it as a perversion, a pagan abomination, is consistent throughout the OT (Lev 18:22; 20:13; 1 Kgs 14:24; 15:12; 22:46; 2 Kgs 23:7), with the sin of Sodom often recalled as a terrible warning (e.g., Gen 19:1-28; Deut 23:18; Isa 1:9-10; 3:9; Jer 23:14; Lam 4:6; Ezek 16:43-58). In the period of early Judaism, abhorrence of homosexuality is not just part of the reaction against Greek mores, since we find it also in those most influenced by Greek thought (Wisd Sol 14:26; *Ep. Arist.* 152; Philo, *Philo* 135-37; *Spec. Leg.* 3.37-42; *Sib. Or.* 3:184-86, 764; Ps. Phoc. 3, 190-92, 213-14; Josephus, *Ap.* 2.273-75); note also the sustained polemic against sexual promiscuity and homosexuality in *T. 12 Patr.* (particularly *T. Lev.* 14.6; 17.11; *T. Naph.* 4.1) and in *Sib. Or.* (e.g., 3.185-87, 594-600, 763); see further Str-B, 3:68-74. In other words, antipathy to homosexuality remains a consistent and distinctive feature of Jewish understanding of

---

8. Mounce, *Romans*, 80-81.

what man's createdness involves and requires. That homosexuality is of a piece with idolatry is taken for granted (as several of the same passages show), both understood as a demeaning of the people who indulge in them. The link between man's fall (Gen 3) and sexual perversion (as here) is also typically Jewish, since Gen 6:1–4 also played a considerable part in Jewish attempts to account for the origin of sin (*Jub.* 4.22; 5.1–10; 7.21; *1 Enoch* 6–11; 86; *T. Reub.* 5; *T. Naph.* 3.5; CD 2.18–21; etc.). Elsewhere in the NT see 1 Cor 6:9; 1 Tim 1:10; 2 Pet 2; Jude 7.[9]

Both of these exegetical analyses of Rom 1:26–27, categorize homosexuality as a sin regardless of the theological stance. The biblical text itself categorizes same-sex relationships as sin from God's viewpoint or perspective of same-sex relations. However, the text does not dictate the church community's response or specify how the community should relate to same-sex relationships in the church. Both texts simply demonstrate how God sees the behavior and give a theological position as to why the behavior exists and is tolerated.

Jeffress's response is alarming not in the sense of categorizing same-sex relationships as sin. His stance is not about biblical understanding of same-sex relationships; its more so about the church's attitude toward same-sex relationships. Furthermore, whilst there are no clear texts that decry same-sex marriage there are identifiable texts that negate same-sex marriage. The SBC for the most part has built an argument against heterosexual relationships based on the verses of Gen 2:17–24 which are against same-sex relationships. Matthews offers a detailed counter argument to the SBC position:

> The creation of the first couple leads naturally to their relationship expressed through marriage since it is the couple's charge to procreate and subdue the earth (1:28). This verse is not the continued speech of the man but the commentary of the narrator, which is attributed to God by Jesus (Matt 19:4–5). "For this reason" (*'al kēn*) does not indicate an explanation of the foregoing but rather describes the consequence of God's charge for the human family to propagate and rule. Marriage and family are the divine ideal for carrying out the mandate. As we noted, Jesus' appeal to the garden (quoting Gen 2:23) as the basis of his teaching on marriage and divorce (Matt 19:3–9; Mark 10:2–12) indicates that the garden established a paradigm for marital behavior. That Eden was viewed by the Hebrews as the model, authoritative experience can be seen also in Jewish literature of the time but especially by Paul, who appeals to its events in speaking

9. Dunn, *Romans 1–8*, 64–66.

> of the most profound theological tenets of Christianity (Rom 5:12–21; 1 Cor 15:45) and in offering instructions concerning the propriety of worship (1 Cor 11:2–16; 1 Tim 2:11–15), moral behavior (1 Cor 6:16), and marriage (Eph 5:31).
>
> As a model for marriage this passage involves three factors: a leaving, a uniting, and a public declaration. The NIV's rendering *"will* leave" is ambiguous (also NASB); it can be taken by the modern reader as a description of future behavior or as an exhortation to marry. Better is the rendering "leaves" and "clings" (NRSV), indicating by the simple present tense that marriage is a universal practice. Marriage is depicted as a covenant relationship shared by man and woman. Monogamy is clearly intended. "Leave" (⊠*āzab*) and "cling" *(dābaq)* are terms commonly used in the context of covenant, indicating covenant breach (e.g., Deut 28:20; Hos 4:10) or fidelity.[10]

This exposition in the SB New American Commentary states that the biblical marriage is between man and woman and consists of monogamous commitment to each other. Interestingly, Matthews engages the reader with New Testament texts about marriage and morality to elucidate his argument about the primacy and paradigmatic model of marriage as the divine ideal for developing and maintaining the family structure.

Furthermore, SB expositors argue that since marriage is a covenantal relationship, divorce was never a part of God's biblical plan and was only permissible because of the fallibility and hardness of humanity's heart and mindset. According to SB expositors, the divine textual ideal is for the permanency of marriage and divorce perpetrated outside of infidelity, and abandonment of a spouse is a sin. However, the biblical stance is that infidelity and even abandonment may be borne without divorce.

A survey of the biblical teaching on divorce reveals in Matt 19:6 that marriage should not be ended based on sheer human preference, Mal 2:15–16 states that God hates divorce and in the Old Testament adultery would result in death by stoning, although a man was allowed to divorce his wife, the wife was not allowed to divorce her husband for any reason. Legally the wife was bound to her husband as long as they both lived or until he divorced her (1 Cor 7:39).[11] Therefore, divorce outside of abandonment and infidelity is considered a sin according to the text.

Therefore, Jeffress's response to same-sex marriage and his almost venomous disdain for it is somewhat hypocritical as the text comes out equally strongly against divorce as well. However, Jeffress is typical of the

---

10. Mathews, *Genesis 1–11:26*, 222.
11. Youngblood, *Nelson's New Illustrated Bible Dictionary*.

conservative arm of the SBC, notwithstanding all if not most of the SBC churches deny the legitimacy of same sex marriage. The more moderate or liberal SBC congregations may demarcate between the biblical command to love one's neighbor and the traditional biblical concept of marriage between a man and woman. However, they consistently maintain the sinfulness of same-sex marriage but at the same time they are carefully receptive to gays, lesbians, and transgender individuals or couples attending and worshipping in their churches. According to the SBC their disdain of same-sex marriage is based on their objective interpretational examination of the biblical text. The SBC upholds their views and believes that they have a divine right to influence culture and the government to side with their perspective because of their belief that they are following the divine order based on their self-understanding of the interpretation of the text. Furthermore, at the heart of the debate for these churches and SBC congregations is their claim of the redefinition of the literal scriptural rendering of the nature of marriage and the literal directives that warn against same-sex behavior. Whilst it is true that they eschew any form of vindictive or penal castigation for same-sex marriage or homosexual behavior, they clearly identify homosexuality its practices or lifestyle as being against the textual revelation. Literal expositions or expository preaching and the homiletic process all engineer a likely outcome of the impermissibility of gay and lesbian lifestyles. All literal renderings or expositions through the expository method interpret the biblical texts to mean that congregants should not participate in any gay, lesbian or transgender lifestyle. For SBC leaders, theologians and congregants there is no middle ground. Traditional SBC churches consider and articulate a position in which gays, lesbians, and transgender people cannot profess allegiance to and follow Christ and continue to be a member with full rights and privileges of their local SB churches.

Influence on Government and the Economy

The SBC has influenced modern culture because of its irrepressible commitment to the literal understanding of the text based on their exegetical and expositional framework. SBC is generally suspicious of social and cultural trends as well as any political or legal change to historical conservative ideals. The SBC expect that culture including governmental laws and persons's general behavioral attitudes will increasingly flout basic traditional biblical values. This is not to invite these theological aversions in contemporary culture or to flaccidly succumb to social changes without voicing or challenging these ideas. Hence, in modern times the SBC has long considered the

Democratic Party as chiefly responsible for the despoliation of marriage and the family in the larger culture. The convention has consistory qualms with the changing social norms especially abortion and sexuality. The Clinton and Obama administrations, namely President Obama, ignited outrage by supporting LGBT individuals and same-sex marriage.

SBC pulpits and their commitment to expository preaching treaded the balance between honoring government and disparaging the Obama administration's quest for LGBT rights. It not surprising that SBC congregants in more recent times, namely the twenty-first century, are more committed to the Republican Party by hoping a Republican president with political stances like Reagan, Bush, or Trump would nominate conservative Supreme Court judges to elongate the SBC's evangelistic and social influence, delay the subsequent judgment of God, and allow more time to evangelize prospective adherents to their tenets. This argument explains the SBC's commitment to and support of President Trump despite some of his controversial activities. Of note, Trump as a candidate was supported by Senior Pastor Richard Jeffress of FBC Dallas due to Trump's conservative stance on same-sex marriage, abortion, immigration, and other conservative issues.[12]

The SBC has been very stringent in propagating its theological stances based on its exposition of the Bible. The SBC has gone to great lengths to use its theological beliefs to mobilize its congregants to use their economic position to influence culture. For instance, they have utilized the expository method to invigorate their demands that the marriage is defined as the union between a man and woman. The SBC's statement on sexuality states:

> We affirm God's plan for marriage and sexual intimacy—one man, and one woman, for life. Homosexuality is not a "valid alternative lifestyle." The Bible condemns it as sin. It is not, however, unforgivable sin. The same redemption available to all sinners is available to homosexuals. They, too, may become new creations in Christ.[13]

The SBC based their stance on their interpretation of the biblical text and so sought to influence its congregations and national corporations to side with their interpretative understanding of the issue. Accordingly, the SBC to the unique to step to admonish Disney to change its organizational support of anti-Christian themes and gay and lesbian values. The SBC warned Disney to enact changes within a year or else risk that outright boycott that last for eight years when it eventually happened.

---

12. Martin, "Pastor Robert Jeffress Explains."
13. SBC, "Position Statements."

To enact the Disney boycott, the SBC partnered with several church denominations and parachurch organizations. In August 1997, when the boycott began, the SBC claimed it involved nearly twenty million SBC members. Additionally, a week after the boycott began Disney's Hollywood Records recalled over one hundred thousand copies of hip hop group Insane Clown Posse's album "The Great Malenko" due to its offensive lyrics. Also, its share values dropped 8 percent from a May high of $84.50 per share. During the boycott, Disney's animated film "Hercules" did not perform at the nation's theaters as well as Disney had expected. Furthermore, the Catholic League for Religious and Civil Rights joined the boycott along with several other religious denominations, parachurch organizations, and religious special interest groups. SBC and other religious protesters distributed pamphlets at the gates of Disney World and promoted ongoing news releases sent to the financial sector and new media. The SBC continued preaching against Disney in its local churches. In an unusual move by a governmental agency, Texas's state school board sold $46.4 million in Disney stock that had been held in the Texas Permanent School Fund to support the conservative public outcry led by the SBC.[14]

Admittedly, there is no fixed report on the actual negative financial loss suffered by Disney. Many considered that the denomination's stance was nothing more than posturing as an "economic paper tiger," and the Orlando Sentinel found that only thirty percent of SB congregants participated in the boycott.[15] Disney did experience a downturn in its ABC television network ratings, movie-ticket sales, retail outlets, and various theme parks, throughout the eight-year period. Meanwhile, the national economy experienced multiple recessions, terrorist attacks at soft targets like amusement parks and festivals, and general declines in universal viewing of traditional television programming due to the emergence of Internet entertainment streaming services. Some see the social and cultural effect of the SBC's theological and social carriage can be viewed as a failed attempt to influence the national narrative social and biblical values. Notwithstanding the coalition of churches, the print and digital media attention gained by the SBC through their efforts did strengthen the SBC's self-belief as a conservative moral and social voice that can combat the nation's progressive, liberal culture.

---

14. MacDonald and McDonald, "Case Study."
15. Pinsky, *Gospel According to Disney*, 259.

Pro-Israel Support

The SBC has maintained a position of expositional truth that it used when attempting to influence culture and society coercively. The SBC has sought for national recognition of its biblical position and to use its influence over governmental appointees and politicians to enact legislation which protects or imposes its biblical beliefs on the nation.

Once such area on which the SBC has actively sought to have influence is ideology of supporting Israel. Israel's lands hold the biblical position as God's chosen nation. Based on SBC exposition of the Old Testament and New Testament, Israel serves as the pivotal location in future history as the holy nation that must be protected at all costs. A literal reading of Gen 12:1–3 implies that the nations supporting Israel experience blessings or divine success that include specifically economic wealth, military prowess, and social stability. Therefore, SB theologians and pastors are adamant about successive governmental administrations supporting Israel in every way possible. Failure to support Israel will bring about irreparable harm. The SBC has always been a staunch supporter of Israel and pro-Israel policies.

Historically, the SBC supported government administrations and policies by lobbying through special interest groups that uphold the idea that Israel is seminal to realized eschatology at the end of times and related to the inauguration of the God's role on earth. Also, there is the notion that in the here and now represents unrealized eschatology, Israel remains God's token nation. Nations that support Israel will be hallowed and prosperous. SB theologians and pastors have historically involved themselves in witnessing the miracles and teachings of Christ to Jews and winning the cooperation of Christians for the unflinching commitment to evangelizing Jews.[16] The SBC has been committed historically to premillennial dispensationalism, from which its sources appear in literal readings of the biblical prophecies, and to the engineering of the end times as a product of the division of breaking up of time into discrete phases or covenantal time periods related to God's redemptive work, in which Jews appear as the very centerpiece of God's end-of-times drama.[17]

No other SB theologian or pastor has taken a stand for the nation of Israel through his sermons and public platform as has Jerry Falwell. Falwell's affiance with the nation of Israel was one of many seminal roles held by this outspoken, fundamentalist SB leader. Falwell was the founder of the Moral Majority and long considered architect of the religious right movement in

---

16 Cook, "Paul's Argument," 64.
17. Cook, "Paul's Argument," 64.

America.[18] The focuses of the Moral Majority involved ending abortion, promoting traditional gender roles, reinstating public school prayer, and imposing fundamentalist morality on government by influencing laws.[19]

Falwell might have been chiefly responsible for procuring support for and energizing the Republican Party by prompting conservative social values. Falwell is credited with awakening awareness and stimulating congregational attention to various social causes namely homosexuality, abortion, and the separation of the church and state. Falwell's Moral Majority is credited to have helped get Ronald Reagan elected to the US presidency. He was initially an independent Baptist but later joined forces with the SBC in 1996 to devote most of his own time and vivacities toward influencing the political landscape and bringing about social change.

Falwell pastored the Thomas Road Baptists Church and founded Liberty University, both located in Lynchburg, Virginia. Falwell was a literalist in his hermeneutical and homiletic methodology, and even more than Jeffress of FBC Dallas, he ushered his church, congregation and supporters into the realm of political involvement. He used his pulpit to influence culture and politics and established the new ideals of a mega-church. His development of his church would embody his approach to exegesis and homiletics. He formed a church campus with various ministries that catered to social, recreational and spiritual needs dedicated to sports, addiction, early childhood education and employment and personal stewardship.[20] Falwell viewed the church as being intricately and intimately involved in social and political affairs. As a matter of fact, the church serves as the moral compass of culture and society. SB pastors should use their pulpits to steer their congregations toward church polity and encourage congregants to ensure that electoral decisions align with SB biblical preaching.

Falwell's "moral majority" boasted an approach which encompassed "the religious roundtable," which was formed to empower pastors and provide resources for them to inspire their congregations to vote for pro-family and pro-morality candidates. Additionally, in preparation for the 1980 general elections they sponsored mass voter registration, campaign calls informing voters of the morality ratings of each candidate and provided ground transportation to the polls.[21] Through the moral majority Falwell attempted to influence the Reagan administration to bring back public prayers in school, anti-abortion legislation and Supreme Court

---

18. Winters, "God's Right Hand."
19. Tamney and Johnson, "Explaining Support for the Moral Majority," 235.
20. Winters, "God's Right Hand."
21. Buursma, "New Crusade."

appointments. When President Reagan nominated Sandra Day O'Connor, Reagan contacted Falwell and implored him to abstain from public statements until after the Senate hearings. As Cal Thomas publicly questioned her affinity for conservative values, it was recorded that Falwell voiced his displeasure toward Thomas to preserve his open communication channel with President Reagan.[22]

Falwell's reading and exegesis of Scripture was done through the lens of a literal reading based on the expository methodology. Whilst Falwell was not known for strict verse-by-verse expository preaching. His model was that of expositing the literal historical meaning of the text and homiletically conveying the sense of the text to his audience highlighting contemporary connections which were considered veracious for life, culture, and society. In other words, Falwell applied literal injunctions in the Bible based on dispensational location and decrypted its contemporary relevance and significance. His focus on Israel was due to its literal location in the book of Genesis as God's chosen nation and the initial point for God's redemptive work in the world. Therefore, Falwell read biblical references to Israel as historic and deemed references in the Bible yet to occur in time and history as prophetic.

The Israel of the Bible then is a continuance of the Israel of today. The references to Israel are dissimilar to the references to the concept of church in the New Testament and in the modern era. The church is not the new Israel instead the church has been grafted into redemptive history and there is role for Israel in the future redemptive history of the Bible. The references to Israel from Genesis to Revelation and particularly in Gen 12:1–2 when God told Abraham. "I will bless those who bless you, and the one who curses you I will curse. And in you all the families of the earth shall be blessed" (Gen 12:3), is relevant and true for all times. Falwell connected America's prosperity with her support of Israel. Falwell's hermeneutic influenced his sermonic support for socially conservative policies and political candidates. He funneled financial resources to lobbyist and electoral campaigns in an effort to shape culture. He utilized his media broadcast to endorse or admonish social and political figures. His approach and role in the SBC launched or induced a philosophy whereby the local church without being a purely social gospel movement now represented and disseminated ideals which were definitively based on a literal, historical-grammatical reading of the text. Falwell's and other SBC pastors's methodology was based on system of identifying literal renderings in the text and assessing its relation to biblical and contemporary culture whether there were purely ceremonial or social laws given to Israel or the Law was abrogated or extended in the New Testament.

22. Marley, "Ronald Reagan," 858.

The issue for the SBC theologians rarely was the veracity of its occurrence in the text but its significance for the contemporary audience. The SBC adherents then had a built-in confidence and sure-footedness that their preaching was superior and that their sermonic ideals were expressing the words and mind of God. This undoubtedly led to their support of so many social, biblical conservative values including their support of Israel. The SBC through their hermeneutic and homiletic viewpoint has long supported causes sermonically and financially along with other like-minded institutions to ensure that their biblical values are immersed and embrace in common culture.

Pro-Life, Anti-Abortion Advocacy

Abortion too remained a lugubrious subject for the SBC. It has consistently maintained that the scriptural text when exposited literally and proclaimed from using an expository homiletic model indicates that abortion is not biblical. Russell Moore, SBC theologian and ethicist has analyzed this issue showing the evolving theological understanding of this issue and the subsequent benefaction of anti-abortion policies. Russell Moore chronicles the embryonic understanding and change of viewing abortion. He shows how the SBC eventually followed the Roman Catholic view of abortion even discussing Criswell's reversal of his biblical position to becoming anti-abortionist. Moore suggests that the shift in Criswell's position and that of the SBC was symbiotically inaugurated with conservative resurgence and the amplified engrossed appeal to biblical inerrancy. Many SB leaders viewed the Roe vs. Wade Supreme Court's decision to allow for abortion as an illicit approval for rampant killing of unborn fetus. With the amplified concern for unborn babies, the growing suspicion of the Supreme Court and a renewed emphasis on biblical and exposition of the texts regarding abortion therewith led to the resultant change. The change in outlook by the SBC which is now ardently pro-life has led to a continued support of pro-life causes and lobbying for pro-life legislations, especially in the Southern United States. Sermonic material in most SB churches and seminaries indicate a cohesive and fervent pro-life impulse and ongoing financial support for pro-life causes. The shift in positions began the process whereby new resolutions were introduced at the annual SBC conference that essentially documented their fulgent evolution of their stringent pro-life ideology. The SBC has partnered with pro-life agencies and para-church organizations have invested heavily in pro-life causes. However, their support of this cause and evolving approach has revealed a salient but elusive hermeneutical stratagem which they have not fully employed or embraced. Their hermeneutical process involves the exegetical study of the original language, grammar, syntax, genre and historical context and their homiletics attempts to parlay the application and personal application of the themes under examination. However, Criswell's dawdling nascent methodological views on abortion could have been abetted by the inclusion of teleological exegetical study. This approach is connected to canonical theology in that it investigates a subject matter from its first occurrence in the biblical text and seeks to chart the theological revelation and development of the subject in the text based on its historical occurrence in the text. Hence a teleological exegetical study in this sense would look at how the text treated the idea of human life and death and the Bible's understanding of the body when studying the topic of abortion. SB scholar and theologian writes about abortion and the biblical stance utilizing the canonical approach from a historical or teleological standpoint:

> With this emphasis, evangelical theology has reclaimed a more biblical portrait of the holistic and cosmic nature of redemption. Evangelicals do not have biblical warrant to disengage from the life-and- death issues of the public square in order to pursue an "other-worldly" and "wholly spiritual" endeavor of rescuing souls from the created order. The Christian doctrine of salvation is rooted in the creation purposes of God, as well as in the eschatological *telos* of creation in the restoration of the image of God (Rom 8:29) and the regeneration of the entire cosmos (Eph 1:10). The two come together in the resurrection of Jesus from the dead, the decisive act of redemptive history that confirms the Kingdom purposes of God for the whole of humanity, body and soul, as well as for the whole of the created order. The resurrection of Jesus, as the righteous human firstborn of the new creation (Col 1:18; Heb 5:7–9) along with the future resurrection of the Messiah's joint-heirs is a resounding confirmation that God still deems His cosmos—including His justified image-bearers—as "good" (Rom 8:19–23). This informs evangelical engagement on issues such as abortion because, as ethicist Oliver O'Donovan observes, the resurrection does away with any notion that Christian theology mandates a negation of the bodily and material aspects of created reality.[23]

Moore's point is that a thorough exegetical analysis of the text from Genesis to Revelation reveals that the text is concerned with both body and soul and that Jesus's bodily resurrection cements the textual concern with a

23. Moore, "Gospel According to Jane Roe," 44–45.

soteriological understanding that humanity converges in body and soul and that any bifurcation limits humanity or goes against the biblical standard. Hence, the moment there is conception regardless of the state of the body, according to Moore and SB there is life and the existence of personhood. Moore contends, "By envisioning the mission of the Kingdom as encompassing concern for both body and soul, and by seeing Kingdom priorities as including both the justification of the wicked and justice for the innocent, evangelical theology might have been better prepared for the cultural upheaval that led to the debate over abortion rights"[24] Questions regarding abortion, when life begins would be answered by utilizing the canonical approach and its focus on the teleological or systematic development of the theological idea of abortion.

Maintaining Contemporary Relevance

The SBC has also endorsed and financially supported issues that fit its mode of viewing the culture through its interpretative scheme. It is noteworthy that there are groups that oppose the values of the SBC and therewith are correspondingly financially vested in influencing political and social arena. The SBC does not contribute specifically to social justice causes but instead contends with the political leaders, corporations, presidential administrations when a public policy contradicts its biblical social values. It appears that when governmental or corporate policies controvert expository sermonic teachings or literal readings of the scriptural texts about the traditional conservative family structure, the complementarian role of women, traditional gender roles, and national financial stability or prosperity there is a theological upheaval and congregational angst. This eventually leads to financial support and preaching to awaken awareness and bring about change.[25]

The SBC has armed itself with several entities to influence, proliferate and express its spiritual and social values and protect its ministers. The most potent arm of the SBC from a congregational standpoint and for equipping its ministers, churches and transmitting its spiritual values is its LifeWay Christian Resources. The SBC like most major denominations aspires to educate and inform its congregants through the production and dissemination of its own theological materials in hopes that it will protect its denominational stances and protect its congregants from disparate theological social and spiritual values. The SBC through its churches, seminaries and entities is able to continue the development of pastors and churches and maintain

24. Moore, "Gospel According to Jane Roe," 44–45.
25. Pew Research Center, "Religious Advocacy Group."

a media presence as it seeks to preserve its social and spiritual values. It is mainly through its pulpits, churches such as FBC Dallas, Prestonwood Church, Cross Church, and Thomas Road Baptist Church. One of the most influential pastors and churches is Saddleback Church. It is one of the largest churches in the United States and has considerable influence with many world leaders and American presidential administration. These churches and their leaders continue to convey social and spiritual values which reflect conservative, traditional biblical ideals. Rick Warren, pastor of Saddleback church has authored *The Purpose Driven Church* in 1995 and *The Purpose Driven Life* in 2002, with the latter going on to sell thirty million copies worldwide, becoming one of the highest Christian best-sellers in the world, as well as one of the most translated books after the Bible. He along with SBC theologians and leaders have lend financial support to many social and political causes in an effort to ensure that culture reflects or experiences their biblical values.

The SBC has made inroads and has strong financial influence in the governmental and social arena through their pulpit proclamations, publications, seminaries and its numerous entities. Its expository method continues to be a tool or framework used to support socially conservative ideas that receive support and impetus due to public reactions to social change in the family structure, societal reactions to perceived negative behaviors such gambling, abortion same-sex marriage and even immigration. SB maintain a commitment to the theological belief in inerrancy and inspiration and that their pastors, theologians and leaders ascribe to framework where they are applying the scriptural text according to its divine intended meaning. SB leaders have long argued that their exegetical and homiletic methodology is focused on inductive deriving the actual meaning of the texts and so are conveying the actual words that God wanted congregants to hear.

Therefore, the SBC pastors and theologians were truthful and precise in their values and social beliefs. They were acting on or living according to the scriptural text, the very words of God. Their system of interpreting the text then was without theological bias or self-imposed biblical ideals. According to their expository preaching model and literal interpretation of biblical text their social and ecclesiological viewpoints where biblically and theological informed and represented God's view of what culture and society should be. It appears that the vulnerability of the SBC is not its claim to the advocacy and practice of the literal interpretation and proclamation of the scriptural texts but instead its overt involvement in the political landscape. In that the SBC will need to have a more balanced approach and not only seem value about specific hot-button issues but be more devoted to expository teaching about all of life's issue and be more concerned about the general well-being of congregants and the community.

The problem with SB according to one SB scholar and theologian is that they have become "defensive and reactionary."[26] Akin believes that they have lost their evangelistic fervor, commitment to the family, missionary zeal among other things. Akin believes that the SB churches should focus on systematically teaching the doctrines of the Bible instead of reacting to hot button issues that come up in culture. Akin states, "We must teach doctrine, love doctrine, and proclaim doctrine."[27] Akin's approach has been practiced by W. A. Criswell who preached systematically through the Bible beginning in 1946 with Genesis and after 17.5 years he finished Revelation. Allen writes about the growth of the church during this time period:

> Under Dr. Criswell's preaching, FBC became the prototype for the mega-church with her membership rolls swelling to over 25,000 by the mid-1980s. In an era when preaching in the main-line denominational churches was afflicted with nervous prostration, Criswell proved you could build a great church on the expositional preaching of the Bible as the inerrant Word of God.[28]

It seems that the best approach would be to address hot button issues through the expository preaching methodology but have a consistent plan to teach through the books of the Bible. Criswell wrote about his plan to preach through the Bible and alluded to the freedom and focus that it brought:

> For eighteen years I preached through the Bible. I began at the first verse in Genesis and continued through the last verse in the Revelation. Where I left off in the morning, I picked up in the evening, and thus every Sunday, morning and evening, I followed the message of the Holy Scriptures. God blessed the procedure more than I could ever have hoped. The response of the people was amazing to me. When I began the series, some of the most discerning church members said I would empty the house of the Lord. Nobody, they said, would continue to come to the services and listen to messages that waded through all those so-called dreary and empty chapters of the Bible. But God had placed it on my heart to begin preaching through the Bible. The result is a finished story. So many people began coming to God's house that after a while they could not be packed in, although

---

26. Akin, "Future of Southern Baptists," 81.
27. Akin, "Future of Southern Baptists," 81.
28. Allen, "Preaching, Leading."

the auditorium is one of the most spacious in America. We finally had to begin holding two morning services. Now, at both hours the auditorium is filled. Our people began bringing their Bibles, reading their Bibles, studying their Bibles. They began witnessing to others as never before. More and more souls were saved. The spirit of revival and refreshment became the daily order in the house of the Lord. It was the greatest experience of my life. Often I have seen preachers pace up and down the floors of their studies, trying to figure out what they would preach about the next Sunday. I have also found myself pacing up and down, perplexed over the sermon for the following Sunday. But our problems were different. Theirs was what to preach about, where to find a text, what to say. Mine was how to say all . . .[29]

The SBC has been quick to focus on issues that fall within a smaller category of hot-button issues instead covering the various theological and societal issues in the biblical text. When issues such as immigration become cultural, the SBC focuses on these issues to the detriment of other textual ideologies. Therefore, it seems that SB is driven by issues that are critical to political, family, or socially conservative issues instead of being driven to teach and preach the doctrines in the Bible.

It is because of this approach that the SBC has developed a reputation of being pro-Republican even when electoral candidates are deemed to be without Christian values. This perspective about the SBC has limited its ability to broaden its reach to minority groups and to be more representative of diverse cultures. The moral majority being disappointed with President Jimmy Carter (who was a SB at the time of his presidency) helped elect Ronald Reagan and George H. W. Bush. Bill Clinton claimed to be SBC and was duly elected and supported by the SBC who later expressed an utter sense of disappointment due to his adulterous behaviors. President George W. Bush, though not a member of the SBC, would later garner widespread support from evangelicals and the SBC.

The SBC has tended to support Republican candidates in the twenty-first century, and specifically, has endorsed candidates who were directly affiliated with the SBC or who were overtly evangelical. The SBC, through a commitment to the Bible and literal interpretation of the scriptural text, has historically valued personal evangelism, baptism, and foreign missions. The SBC's ministry goals involves growing its membership through evangelism and baptism and developing a pedagogical and discipleship process that creates a sense of commitment by adherents to their local churches. Furthermore, SBC leaders are historically ardent supporters of investing in

29. Olsen, "Southern Baptist Leaders."

their local churches and educationally equipping young pastors to become effective communicators and moral pastoral caregivers. The SBC is also known for its zealous involvement in foreign and local missions as well as for raising and investing significant sums to evangelize non-Christian nations and peoples. The SBC has experienced some loss in membership and political influence.

SBC scholars and theologians like Akin have argued that the SBC must deepen its resolve and focus on its own biblical and theological narrative of evangelization, baptism and discipleship. Its own expository and theological model endorses the belief that the purpose and existence of the SBC and its churches lies in its mission and visionary values in Matt 28:18–20, the Great Commission textual reference. He also asserts that the SBC must methodically rebuild its image but more than that it must reestablish its theological roots as a denomination that is primarily focused on expositing biblical teachings and showing its relevance for personal daily living. He argues too that the requirements for membership should be connected with authentic biblical regeneration and biblical pedagogical instruction and that the congregation should be taught true SBC theology and which represent a clear and complete allegiance to Baptist theology will be more adherent and effective in influencing culture. Therewith, a SBC congregation that reflects a membership that fully understands and accepts its theological roots and which has been individually and personally metamorphosed biblically, will be fervent evangelists, missionary oriented and will convert or proselytize more followers and hence increase its congregational size and appeal.[30]

In an interview prior to his election as SBC president during the 2016 SBC annual meeting in St. Louis Missouri, Steve Gaines outlined his concerns and the necessary changes the SBC must make in order to remain true to its historic, traditional biblical tenets and to effectively influence culture. He called for a spiritual awakening where there is a demonstrable love for people:

> When Jesus was asked, what is the greatest commandment is, He said, quoting from the Shema, love the Lord your God and love people (Deuteronomy 6:4–6). That is the essence of what happens when God sends a spiritual awakening. There's an enhanced love for God which always results in a love for people. Whenever you love the Lord you're going to love the people that He created in His image. . .And so I want a spiritual awakening. So I'm praying that God would pour out His Spirit upon our churches. That's what I think we need. I think that is the reason

---

30. Akin, "Future of Southern Baptists," 83.

we are not baptizing. The baptisms are just the evidence of the fact that we're not as much in love with Jesus and in love with people as we need to be. So spiritual awakening is a big thing.[31]

Gaines apparently recognizes the need to re-engage culture. However, the call to love seems to be a strategic goal in enamoring his peers to love people. He is concerned with increasing conversions or specifically baptisms and not really with the personal betterment of one's life or living situation. Gaines continues his observation about lack of baptisms and determines that there is a lack of "soul winning" or personal evangelism in SBC churches. Gaines belabors his point and reasserts the need to personally invite and intentional win over converts in culture. Gaines argues for personally engaging culture and leading people to believe and accept their biblical message. Russell Moore suggests that the SBC must not be afraid to engage contemporary culture and must avoid isolationism and condemnations. He accepts the changing fabric of culture and appeals to SBC churches to point their efforts at preaching, evangelizing but to expect the conflict to come because of the content of the preaching but not through the behavioral, loveless attitude of SBC adherents. It makes the point too that the ultimate realization of their biblical ideas lies in the eschatological experience of the kingdom of God. Moore, constructs a picture of preaching amidst a hostile cultural storm but that SBC leaders, theologians and members should fearlessly embrace and extend their care and consideration towards contemporary culture in hopes of spreading their message and doctrine:

> The temptation for future generations of Baptist conservatives is probably not that they will be too consumed by the "culture wars." The temptation will be to surrender to the seeming omnipotence of "McWorld." The next generation of Baptists was not reared in the isolated subculture of "Sword Drills" and "Acteen" camp. They will come of age in the cultural atmosphere of a new moralism—with Planned Parenthood preaching "safety" in their public school classrooms and *Will and Grace* preaching "tolerance" on the network airwaves. Moreover, they may find that the future of the conservative resurgence is not chiefly in middle-class suburban America, but in the persecuted congregations of the Third World. There is, after all, little appeal to a "moderate" Baptist social gospel when claiming Christ means literal crucifixion by a despotic Islamic government.[32]

---

31 Staff, "Vision for the Future."
32. Moore, "Resurgence vs. McWorld," 43–44.

The SBC then is wanting to ensure that as denomination they remain relevant in contemporary society without compromising its theological integrity or doctrinal dogma. As Moore outlined, SBC leaders expect to have growth in the SBC but only through the maintenance of the doctrinal purity. The SBC view many practices in contemporary culture as detrimental to the nation and the world at large in addition to SBC congregants via apocalyptic images of "Babylon," which conjure up pictures of an evil nation and the risk of judgment.

The SBC sees it role as expositors from a theological as well as a social perspective. They view their belief system as vital to protecting culture and through the preaching and publication of literal translations that they can effectively influence and mobilize culture to accept and appreciate SBC dogma. On a deeper level the SBC attempts to preserve their denomination from liberalism and contradictory dogma through their preaching and lobbying efforts. Their ability to mobilize their congregations have shown their economic power albeit somewhat limited but still able to influence politics and society. In the end they argue their goal is the preservation of culture but too it appears that they are intent of preservation their denomination and to accelerate its growth and influence in the United States and the world at large.

Use of Media

The SBC has used the radio and television to impart its social conservative message and to influence culture. Integral to the scope and involvement of the SBC social conservative message has the work of James Dobson, founder of Focus on the Family in 1977 and which he led until 2003. Dobson later founded "Family Talk" a similarly socially conservative radio talk show that focusses on traditional family values, the complementarian role of women, public prayers in school, he opposes same-sex marriage and cohabitation of heterosexuals and homosexuals. Dobson has been lauded by SB leaders as the *sine qua non* of the social conservative movement in particularly in American suburbia and in religious conservative circles. Through his work at "Focus on the Family" and "Family Talk," Dobson has influenced several political administrations and successfully fought against several progressive and liberal legislations. He has used his radio broadcast to lament and galvanize support for conservative causes which he felt were eroding biblical standards and as such he garnered widespread support from the SBC. Dobson supported the boycott of Disney and has spoken at the SBC annual meeting. His readership and listenership through FOF include 3000 outlets in the United States and 40 countries, including newsletters, magazines and websites. His program was also aired in forty countries and included a ninety-second TV commentary aired by about one hundred stations and numerous network affiliates. Dobson also authored over twenty books including the popular standard bearer, *Dare to Discipline* and he even delved into the film industry. Speaking on the twenty-fifth anniversary of Focus on the Family then President of the SBC and pastor of Prestonwood Baptist Church, Dr. Jack Graham comments,

> I think a generation has been changed, an entire generation of Christians and families have been changed by the biblical and practical counsel and guidance from Dr. Dobson. . .I believe Dr. Dobson to be one of the most influential citizens in the country. He's like a Daniel, who in his own generation has touched the nation with the biblical message, a message of truth.[33]

Dobson reflected at time of his anniversary that society,

> Has split now into two broad camps, in what I would call a civil war of values: . . . God is [and] God isn't. If God is, it changes everything. That's why we believe in the sanctity of life, in the dangers of premarital sex, in sexual loyalty and fidelity, the Ten Commandments, honesty and integrity. There's this whole understanding that influences behavior that comes from that idea that God is, that he exists and his Word is true.

On the other hand, Dobson said, those who believe "God isn't" make up their own rules. Those people leave or abandon what is inconvenient, including babies and elderly family members. "If God doesn't exist, everyone is free to do with life as they wish, including determining that homosexuality is no different, morally, than heterosexuality," he said. "These two world views are in collision," Dobson said. "Values are upside down. It is still a $25,000 fine to kill an eagle's egg, and it's not even a misdemeanor . . . to abort a baby. It's not the equivalent of a parking ticket to do that to a viable healthy baby."[34] Dobson has remained a staunch supporter of the SBC and its social values.

Conclusion

The SBC's historical basis for practicing expository preaching was developed based on hermeneutic principles that began in the Neolithic Bible

---

33. Toalston, "Southern Baptists Laud James Dobson."
34. Toalston, "Southern Baptists Laud James Dobson."

period, continued during the period of antiquity that included the first century, and is currently practiced in contemporary times. The SBC has regurgitated these hermeneutic principles in their seminaries and pulpits as part of mining the historical, inerrant, and infallible truths of biblical texts. SB pastors and theologians focus on the activity of expository preaching because of the underlying notion that personal salvation, sanctification, and transformation result from understanding and accepting the original biblical texts's ideas. Henceforth, the formulated principles practiced by biblical writers, including the historical Jesus and his twelve apostles and foremost SBC theologians.

The principles they adopt focus on accessing the original literal, grammatical, and cultural understanding of the text. SB theologians acquiesce to the idea that only an understanding of the original through the examination of the original Greek, Hebrew, and Aramaic yields an accurate translation and rendition of the original. The underlying idea for the SBC is the intrinsic reliability in the original text, and only through preaching do the tenets and context of the original enable the polity experience personal transformation. This commitment to expository preaching serves as the foundation for the SB practice of preaching, leading local churches and the denomination, using specific translations, and adopting certain ideological and political preferences. Expository preaching with its emphasis on the original text and historical traditional values has led to expositing literal Bible translations in SB churches and promoting ancient, traditional, and conservative beliefs that include the rejection of abortion, gambling, same-sex marriage laws, and gender-neutral translations, and for the most, includes the support of Republican ideologies.

The central figures in the SBC included Daniel Akin (president of Southeastern Seminary), David Allen, (Professor of Theology and Homiletics at Southwestern Seminary), Jim Shaddix (Professor of Preaching at Southeastern Seminary), R. Albert Mohler, Jr. (President of Southern Baptist Theological Seminary; Joseph Emerson Brown (Professor of Christian Theology) and famous historical expository practitioners such as W. A. Criswell, John A. Broadus and Paige Patterson. These individuals have served in SBC pulpits, on SBC faculties and in leadership roles in SBC seminaries. The hallmark of the practice of expository preaching included the utilization of genre analysis to understand specific textual form so as to ensure that the right interpretative model was being use based on the type of genre text in the original. The SBC believe that this practice is paramount for unveiling the original intent of the biblical author even when writing in various literary forms, such as narrative, didactic, or poetry.

Additionally, SB theologians, pastors, and leaders see a correlation between church growth and expository preaching and believe that the best or most effective way to numerically grow the congregation is through expository preaching and hence their undying emphasis on its practice in pulpits and their seminaries. SBC have not only adopted an expository methodology based on the exegetical examination of the text but also have emphasized a homiletic methodology that ensures that the original text is always communicated to the congregants. This practice forms the basis for believing in and developing the SBC's historical, theological, and traditional ideas. They would garner ideas for the original context and through the practice of the preaching historical truths from the Neolithic and first century Christianity in the Bible. SB pastors hold on to historical doctrines and beliefs that can seem outdated in contemporary times.

Furthermore, SBC theologians and pastors have a commitment to certain translations because of their inherent beliefs about congregants needing to read and hear sermonic materials that closely correspond to original autographs of biblical text. Due to their foundational beliefs regarding the theological priesthood of congregants and the ideological concern with inerrancy and verbal plenary inspiration, SBC theologians and pastors have emphasized literal translations of the Bible. Hence, the SBC has resisted the use of translations for preaching, teaching, and personal reading that do not preserve the accuracy or the literalness of the original.

The SBC has invested, through denominational agencies, in formal equivalence translations even though ironically this formal translation impedes ease of use or clarity in personal reading or preaching. Nonetheless, the concern is that translations that do not follow the literalness of the original lead congregants astray from SBC doctrine and dogma and thwart theological consistency amongst congregants and the denomination in general. The SBC prefers that congregants reading a biblical text that, though wooden and literal, correlates tightly and literally with the original but can be read to bring about personal transformation.

The end result of SBC theologians's and pastors's commitment to expository preaching is that they maintain a traditional, theological dogma in their churches and seminaries as well as cultural, ideological stances that in some cases operate against but in other cases influence mainstream culture. The SBC believe in holding to certain conservative values that preserve culture from deviating from historical norms that benefit society in general. The SBC firmly believes that the biblical text in its original autographs are effective in bringing about personal and congregation transformation. Consequently, SBC theologians and pastors strive to exegete and homiletically communicate the original and utilize a literal translation of the text to reinforce perceptions and beliefs in their communication original biblical tenets. This commitment is both to the person and teaching of Jesus and to the fixed, traditional values, regardless of the cultural or legal ramifications in society. The SBC seeks to remain faithful to the original biblical text so its congregations can be identified as truly aligned with the Bible. By doing so, the SBC can be trusted and followed as a denomination because of its methodology which follows both religious and scientifically grounded principles.

Bibliography

Akin, Daniel. "The Essentials for Effective and Engaging Exposition." Lecture presented for the Mullins Lectures at The Southern Baptist Theological Seminary, Louisville, KY, October 5, 2005
———. "A Biblical Model for Preaching the Word of God, Nehemiah 8:1-12." Southeastern Baptist Theological Seminary Chapel Message Delivered by Dr. Akin. October 19, 2005.
———. "A Rapture You Can't Miss, A Judgment You Must Face, A Supper You Will Want to Attend." An Address Given by Dr. Akin at the Acts 1–11 Conference in Lawrenceville, Georgia. November 13, 2009.
———. "The Emerging Church and Ethical Choices: The Corinthian Matrix." In *Evangelicals Engaging Emergent: A Discussion of the Emergent Church Movement*, edited by William D. Henard and Adam W. Greenway. Nashville: Broadman, 2009.
———. "The Future of Southern Baptists: Mandates for What We Should Be in the Twenty First Century." *Southern Baptist Journal of Theology* 9.1 (2005) 81. http://equip.sbts.edu/publications/journals/journal-of-theology/
———. "The Future of the Southern Baptists: Mandates for What We Should Be in the Twenty-First Century." *Southern Baptist Journal of Theology* 9 (2005) 69–71. http://equip.sbts.edu/publications/journals/journal-of-theology/
———. "A Biblical Model for Preaching the Word of God, Nehemiah 8:1-12." Southeastern Baptist Theological Seminary Chapel Message Delivered by Dr. Akin. October 19, 2005.
———. "Southern Baptists, Evangelicals, and the Future of Denominationalism." Address delivered at Union University, Jackson, TN, October 7–8, 2009.
Alexander, T. D., and B. S. Rosner, eds. *New Dictionary of Biblical Theology*. Downers Grove, IL: InterVarsity, 2000.
Allen, Clifton Judson. "Race Relations." *Encyclopedia of Southern Baptists*. Nashville: Broadman, 1982.
Allen, David L. "Preaching and Postmodernism: An Evangelical Comes to the Dance." *Southern Baptist Journal of Theology* 5.2 (2001) 70–78. http://equip.sbts.edu/publications/journals/journal-of-theology/
———. "'With a Bible in My Hand': The Preaching Legacy of W. A. Criswell." https://www.preaching.com/articles/past-masters/with-a-bible-in-my-hand-the-preaching-legacy-of-w-a-criswell/
———. "Text-Driven Preaching and Pragmatic Textual Analysis." https://theologicalmatters.com/2014/01/07/text-driven-preaching-and-pragmatic-textual-analysis/

"Annual of the Southern Baptist Convention: 1968." Nashville: Southern Baptist Convention, 1968.

Aquinas, Thomas. *Summa Theologica*. New York: Benziger Brothers, 1947. https://www.ccel.org/a/aquinas/summa/home.html.

"Baptists: Admission of Guilt." *Time* 91 (1968) 1.

"Baptists Approve 'Race' Statement." *Dallas Morning News* (June 5, 1968) 13.

"Baptists Release Integration Vote." *New York Times* (June 7, 1968) 40.

"Baptist Urges Fight on Racism." *Dallas Morning News* (June 5, 1968) 13.

"Basic Beliefs." *Southern Baptist Convention*. http://www.sbc.net/aboutus/basicbeliefs.asp

Blomberg, C. *Matthew*. Nashville: Broadman & Holman, 1992.

Boyce, James P. *Abstract of Systematic Theology, 1887*. http://www.reformedreader.org/rbb/boyce/aos/toc.htm

———. *Three Changes in Theological Institutions: An Inaugural Address*. Greenville, SC: C.J. Elford's Book and Job, 1856.

Breneman, M. *Ezra, Nehemiah, Esther*. Vol. 10 of *The New American Commentary*. Nashville: Broadman & Holman, 1993.

Broadus, John A. *A Treatise on the Preparation and Delivery of Sermons*. New York: Hodder & Stoughton, 1898.

———. *Memoir of James Petigru Boyce*. New York: A. C. Armstrong and Son, 1893.

Bruce, F. F. *Canon of Scripture*. Downers Grove, IL: InterVarsity, 1988.

Buttrick, David. *Homiletic: Moves and Structures*. Minneapolis: Fortress, 1987.

Buursma, Bruce. "A New Crusade." *Chicago Tribune*, August 31, 1980.

Chafer, L. S. *Systematic Theology*. vol 1. Grand Rapids, MI: Kregel, 1993.

Committee on Bible Translation. *Preface of The New International Version Inclusive Language Edition*. London: Hodder & Stoughton, 1996.

Cook, Michael J. "Paul's Argument in Romans 9–11." *Review and Expositor* 103 (2006) 61. https://doi.org/10.1177%2F003463730610300107

Council on Biblical Manhood and Womanhood. "The Neutering of 'Man' in the NIVI." June 1, 1977. https://cbmw.org/uncategorized/the-neutering-of-man-in-the-nivi

Craddock, Fred. *As One Without Authority*. St. Louis: Chalice, 2001.

Cranfield, C. E. B. *A Critical and Exegetical Commentary on the Epistle to the Romans. International Critical Commentary*. London: T&T Clark, 2004.

"Criswell Rips Integration." *Dallas Morning News* (February 23, 1956), 1.

Criswell, Wallie A. "Address to the Joint Assembly." Wednesday, February 22 1956. Rubenstein Library: Rare Book and Manuscript Collection. Durham: Duke University.

———. "The Church of the Open Door." Delivered 8:15 a.m. on June 9, 1968 at First Baptist Church of Dallas. https://wacriswell.com/sermons/1968/the-church-of-the-open-door.

———. *Why I Preach that the Bible is Literally True*. Nashville: B and H Publishing Group, 1969.

Dagg, J. L. *The Elements of Moral Science*. New York: Sheldon, 1859.

———. *The Evidences of Christianity*. Macon, GA: J. W. Burke and Company, 1869.

———. *Manual of Church Order*. Harrisonburg, VA: Gano Books, 1990.

"Dallas Pastor Challenges Race Integration in Church." *Dallas Times Herald*, February 22, 1956.

"Dallas Pastor Stirs Controversy with Statements on Integration." *The Baptist Message*, March 1, 1956.

Dargan, E. C. "The Baptist Pulpit of the Nineteenth Century: Southern." *A Century of Baptist Achievement*. Edited by A. H. Newman. Philadelphia: American Baptist Publication Society, 1901.

De Waard, Jan and Eugene Nida. *From One Language to Another: Functional Equivalence in Bible Translation*. Nashville: Nelson, 1986.

Dockery, D. "Preaching and Hermeneutics." In *Handbook of Contemporary Preaching*, edited by M. Duduit. Nashville, TN: Broadman, 1992.

Dockery, David, and Roger D. Duke. *John A. Broadus: A Living Legacy*. Nashville: B and H, 2008.

"Dr. Criswell Charges Misrepresentation." *Dallas Morning News*, June 6, 1968.

Dugan, George. "Southern Baptists Approve a Strong Racial Stand." *New York Times*, June 6, 1968.

Duke University Library, Special Collections. "Baptist Leader Blasts Integration as 'Idiocy.'" *The State*, February 22, 1956.

Erickson, Millard. *Christian Theology*. 3rd edition. Grand Rapids: Baker, 2013.

Ethics and Religious Liberty Commission of the Southern Baptist Convention. "SBC's Paige Patterson Calls for Immigration Reform, Care for the Immigrants among Us." erlc.com/resource-library/articles/sbcs-paige-patterson-calls-for-immigration-reform-care-for-the-immigrants-among-us/.

"Fast Facts." *Southern Baptist Convention*. http://www.sbc.net/fastfacts/

Foust, Michael. "Mohler, Draper: TNIV Controversy Makes HCSB Translation Even More Important." *Baptist*, June 12, 2002.

Freeman, Curtis W. "'Never Had I Been So Blind': W. A. Criswell's 'Change' on Racial Segregation." *Journal of Southern Religion* 10 (2007) 1–12.

Fuller, R. T. "Choosing a Translation of the Bible." *Journal of Biblical Manhood and Womanhood* 10 (2005) 56–65.

Gamble, H. Y. "Canonical Formation of the New Testament." In *Dictionary of New Testament Background: A Compendium of Contemporary Biblical Scholarship*, edited by Craig A. Evans, 192. Downers Grove, IL: InterVarsity, 2000.

Gerhart, M. "Generic Competence in Biblical Hermeneutics." *Semeia* 43 (1988) 32.

Goldsworthy, Graeme. "Biblical Theology and Hermeneutics," *SBJT* 10 (2006) 3–16.

———. "Lecture 2: Biblical Theology in the Seminary and Bible College," *The Southern Baptist Journal of Theology* 0.4 (Winter 2008) 31–32.

Grudem, W. A. *Systematic Theology: An Introduction to Biblical Doctrine*. Grand Rapids: Zondervan, 2004.

———. *Evangelical Feminism: A New Path to Liberalism*. Wheaton: Crossway, 2006.

Hanson, R. P. C. *Origen's Doctrine of Tradition*. Cambridge: Cambridge University Press, 2015.

———. "NIV Controversy: Participants Sign Landmark Agreement. Guidelines Adopted for Translation of Gender-Related Language in Scripture." *CBMW News* 2.3 (1997) 1, 3-6.

Hirsch, E. D., Jr., *Validity in Interpretation*. New Haven: Yale University Press, 1967.

Hobswabm, Eric, and Terence Ranger. *The Invention of Tradition*. Cambridge: Cambridge University Press, 2012.

Hodge, Charles. *Systematic Theology*. vol. 1. Oak Harbor, WA: Faithlife, 1997.

"Holman Christian Standard Bible." *Southern Baptist Convention*. http://www.sbc.net/resolutions/1140/on-the-holman-christian-standard-bible

Jeffers, Robert. "The New Moral (Dis)order. First Baptist Dallas.org, First Baptist Dallas." http://www.firstdallas.org/search

Jones, J. Estill. "The New Testament and Southern." *Review and Expositor* 82 (1985) 23. https://doi.org/10.1177%2F003463738508200103

Killingsworth, Blake. "Here I Am, Stuck in the Middle with You: The Baptist Standard, Texas Baptist Leadership, and School Desegregation, 1954 to 1956." *Baptist History and Heritage*, 41 (2006) 78–103.

King, Marty. "LifeWay to Continue Selling NIV: Trustees Select New Leadership." http://www.lifeway.com/Article/News-LifeWay-to-continue-selling-NIV-Trustees-select-new-leadership

Knight, G. W. "The Pastoral Epistles: A Commentary on the Greek Text." In *New International Greek Testament Commentary*, edited by Mark Goodacre and Todd D. Still, 411–12. Grand Rapids: Eerdmans, 1992.

Land, Richard. "Americans Don't Want a Truce on 'Social' Issues." *Wall Street Journal*. https://www.wsj.com/articles/SB10001424052748703300904576178390519502436

Luigo, Luis. "Lobbying for the Faithful: Religious Advocacy Groups in Washington, DC." https://www.pewresearch.org/wp-content/uploads/sites/7/2011/11/Religious Advocacy_web.pdf

Luther, Martin. *D. Martin Luthers Werke. Kritische Gesamtausgabe*. 73 vols. Weimar: Herman Böhlaus Nachfolger, 1883-2009.

MacDonald, Robert, and Katie McDonald. "Case Study: Tragic Kingdom? The Southern Baptist Convention Boycott of Walt Disney." *CBAR* 9 (2014) 45–63.

Manis, Andrew M. "Dying from the Neck Up: Southern Baptist Resistance to the Civil Rights Movement." *Baptist History and Heritage* 34 (1999) 33.

———. *Southern Civil Religions in Conflict: Black and White Baptists and Civil Rights, 1947–1957*. Athens, GA: University of Georgia Press, 1987.

Marley, David J. "Ronald Reagan and the Splintering of the Christian Right." *Journal of Church and State* 48 (2006) 858.

Mathews, K. A. *Genesis 1–11:26*. Vol. 1. Nashville: Broadman and Holman, 1996.

McBeth, H. Leon. *The First Baptist Church of Dallas: Centennial History (1868–1968)*. Grand Rapids: Zondervan, 1968.

Mohler, Albert. "The Making of a Great Bible Translator." http://www.albertmohler.com/2009/09/03/the-making-of-a-great-bible-translation/

Moo, Douglas J., "The Bible and Translation, Fifty Years After James Barr." Paper presented at the 66th annual meeting of the Evangelical Theological Society, San Diego, CA, 2014.

Moody, Dale. *Oral History Interview of Dale Moody*. In *Out of His Treasure*, edited by W.O. Carver, 13. Nashville, TN: Broadman, 1956.

Moore, R. "The Gospel According to Jane Roe: Abortion Rights and the Reshaping of Evangelical Theology." *Southern Baptist Journal of Theology* 7 (2003) 44–45.

Mounce, R. H. *Romans*. Nashville: Broadman & Holman, 1995.

Mueller, William A. *A History of Southern Baptist Theological Seminary*. Nashville: Broadman, 1959.

National Council of Churches. "Yearbook of American and Canadian Churches." Available at: http://www.yearbookofchurches.org/group/687

"New Southern Baptist Leader Fully Backs Open Church Policy." *Houston Chronicle*, June 6, 1968.

Newman, Stewart A. "Newman Letter from Stewart A. Newman to W. A. Criswell, July 18, 1968." North Carolina Baptist Collection: Wake Forest University Library.

Nida, Eugene. *Toward a Science of Translating: With Special Reference to Principles and Procedures Involved in Bible Translating.* Leiden: Brill, 1964.

NIV Translators. "Is the NIV Gender Neutral?" http://www.thenivbible.com/niv-gender-neutral/.

Olford, S. F., and D. L. Olford. *Anointed Expository Preaching.* Nashville, TN: Broadman and Holman, 1998.

Olsen, Ted. "Southern Baptist Leaders So Upset About TNIV That Denomination May Abandon NIV." *Christianity Today,* January 1, 2002.

Osborne, Grant R. "Genre Criticism: *Sensus Literalis.*" *Trinity Journal* 4 (1983) 1–27.

———. *The Hermeneutical Spiral: A Comprehensive Introduction to Biblical Interpretation.* Downers Grove, IL: InterVarsity, 1991.

Patapios, Hieromonk. "The Alexandrian and the Antiochene Methods of Exegesis: Towards a Reconsideration." *GOTR* 44 (1999) 259.

Pinsky, Mark I. *The Gospel According to Disney.* Louisville, KY: Westminister John Knox, 2004.

"Position Statements: Women in Ministry." *Southern Baptist Convention.* http://www.sbc.net/aboutus/positionstatements.asp

"Preface." *Holman Christian Standard Bible.* Nashville: Holman Bible, 2009.

Roach, David. "Patterson Denies Mishandling 'Reported Abuse.'" *Baptist.* http://www.bpnews.net/51039/patterson-denies-mishandling-reported-abuse

Roach, E. "Until 1950s, the King James Version Was 'the Bible.'" *Baptist News,* May 5, 2011.

Robertson, Archibald T. *Types of Preachers in the New Testament.* New York: George H. Doran Company, 1922.

———. *An Introduction to the Textual Criticism of the New Testament.* 2nd edition. Oregon: Wipf and Stock, 2014.

———. *Grammar of the Greek New Testament in Light of Historical Research,* London: Hodder and Stoughton, 1919.

———. *The Minister and His Greek New Testament.* London: Hodder and Stoughton, 1923.

———. *Types of Preachers in the New Testament.* New York: George H. Doran Company, 1922.

Ryken, Leland, James Wilhoit, and Tremper Longman III. *Dictionary of Biblical Imagery.* Downers Grove, IL: InterVarsity, 2000.

Schreiner, Thomas R. "Preaching and Biblical Theology." *Southern Baptist Journal of Theology* 10 (2006) 17–29.

———. *Romans.* Baker Exegetical Commentary on the New Testament. Grand Rapids, MI: Baker, 1998.

Shurden, Walter B. "Southern Seminary in the Life of the Southern Baptist Convention." *Review and Expositor* 81 (1984) 394.

"Southern Baptist Resolution on Today's New International Version, St. Louis, MO, 2002." Southern Baptist Convention: St. Louis, MO, 2002. "Positional Statement about the Scriptures." http://www.sbc.net/aboutus/positionstatements.asp

Southern Baptist Convention.Net. "Resolution on Racial Reconciliation on the 150th Anniversary of the Southern Baptist Convention - SBC.net." Https://Www.sbc.net/, www.sbc.net/resource-library/resolutions/resolution-on-racial-reconciliation-on-the-150th-anniversary-of-the-southern-baptist-convention/.

Spencer, Aída B. "Exclusive Language—Is It Accurate?" *Review and Expositor* 95 (1998) 392.

Staff. "A Vision for the Future of the SBC." http://www.sbclife.net/article/2461/a-vision-for-the-future-of-the-sbc

Storey, John W. *Texas Baptist Leadership and Social Christianity, 1900–1980*. College Station, TX: Texas A&M University Press, 1986.

Tamney, Joseph, and Steven Johnson. "Explaining Support for the Moral Majority." *Sociological Forum* 3, no. 2 (1988) 235.

Thistleton, Anthony. "Hermeneutics." In *Dictionary for Theological Interpretation of the Bible*, edited by Kevin J. Vanhoozer, 106. Grand Rapids, MI: Baker, 2005.

Thomas, Robert, L. "The Principle of Single Meaning." *Master's Seminary Journal* 1 (2002) 157. https://www.tms.edu/m/msj29.1.pdf

Toalston, Art. "12 Evangelical Leaders Voice Bible Translation Consensus." *Baptist*. http://www.bpnews.net/3452/12-evangelical-leaders-voice-bible-translation-consensus

———. "Floyd and Former SBC Presidents Take Marriage Stance." *Baptist*. http://bpnews.net/44950/floyd-and-former-sbc-presidents-take-marriage-stance

———. "Gender-neutral NIV Revision Announced; Bible Society Drops Translation Accord." *Baptist Press*. http://www.bpnews.net/12625/genderneutral-niv-revision-announced-bible-society-drops-translation-accord

———. "Southern Baptists Laud James Dobson, Focus on the Family at 25-Year Mark." *Baptist*. http://bpnews.net/13945/southern-baptists-laud-james-dobson-focus-on-the-family-at-25year-mark.

Toulouse, Mark G. "W. A. Criswell." In *Twentieth-Century Shapers of American Popular Religion*, edited by Charles H. Lippy, 88. Santa Barbara, CA: Greenwood, 1989.

VanGemeren, William A. *New International Dictionary of Old Testament Theology and Exegesis*. 5 vols. Grand Rapids: Zondervan, 2012.

Village Church. "What Is Complementarianism?" http://thevillagechurch.net/

Vines, Jerry and David Allen. "Hermeneutics, Exegesis, and Proclamation." *Criswell Theological Review* 1 (1987) 309.

Wills, George A. *Southern Baptist Theological Seminary 1859–2009*. Oxford: Oxford University Press, 2009.

Winters, Michael Sean. *God's Right Hand: How Jerry Falwell Made God a Republican and Baptized the Religious Right*. New York: Harper Collins, 2012.

Young, Frances M. "Patristic Biblical Interpretation." In *Dictionary for Theological Interpretation of the Bible* edited by Kevin J. Vanhoozer, 567. Grand Rapids, MI: Baker, 2005.

Young, Stephens. "A Guide to Robert Jeffress' Excuses for Donald Trump." *Dallas Observer*, August 31, 2018. https://www.dallasobserver.com/news/robert-jeffress-top-10-excuses-for-donald-trump-11085895

Youngblood, Ronald F., ed. *Nelson's New Illustrated Bible Dictionary*. Nashville, TN: Thomas Nelson, 1995.

www.ingramcontent.com/pod-product-compliance
Lightning Source LLC
Chambersburg PA
CBHW070910160426
43193CB00011B/1421